PARABLES
OF JESUS

The Master's stories of love and grace

LYNDELLE BROWER
CHIOMENTI

Pacific Press Publishing Association
Nampa, Idaho
Oshawa, Ontario, Canada

Edited by Kenneth R. Wade
Designed by Michelle Petz
Cover art by Lars Justinen

Accuracy of all quotations and references is the responsibility of the author.

Chiomenti, Lyndelle Brower, 1950-
    Parables of Jesus : the Master's stories of love and
grace / Lyndelle Brower Chiomenti.
        p.   cm.
    Includes bibliographical references.
    ISBN 0-8163-1376-8 (pbk. : alk. paper)
    1. Jesus Christ—Parables. 2. Christian life. I. Title.
BT375.2.C54 1997
226.8'06—dc21
                                                96-46582
                                                    CIP

97 98 99 00 01 • 5 4 3 2 1

CONTENTS

This book is dedicated to:

J. V. Anderson, who taught me the value of good stories;
G. R. Hill, whose stories inspire faith, hope, and friendship;
P. J. Chiomenti, whose stories daily intertwine with mine;
Silver, whose stories abruptly ended during the writing of
Chapter 6;
Elke, whose stories pick up where Silver's left off;
Christ, whose stories are the greatest ever told.

A WORD OF EXPLANATION

Each chapter of this book is divided into the following sections:

1. *The parable.* Here you will learn a bit more about a certain parable, plus a lot more about a specific subject pertaining to the parable.

2. *Elsewhere in the Bible.* This section highlights a person or group of people in Scripture whose personal stories reflect the lesson of the parable discussed in the first section.

3. *Your story.* People just like yourself have contributed willingly to this part of each chapter. Their personal stories are a case in point, illustrating the material dealt with in sections one and two. Without exception, each of these co-authors expressed the hope that her/his story would encourage all who read this book. It is this author's hope that these stories will encourage all of us to share with others how God has made a difference in our lives. (Every effort has been made to protect the identity of the co-authors and the identity of those people involved in their stories.)

4. *Now what?* All the parables and personal stories reflect God's desire to be active in our lives. What difference will such a desire make in your life? This final section outlines a spiritual discipline (prayer, Bible study, etc.) that, when practiced, will help God realize His desire. Each discipline relates in some way to the specific subject studied in the first three sections.

Because there was not room to quote all scriptural references, you will want to have your Bible with you as you read this book. Unless otherwise noted, all quoted references are from the New International Version. The author in no way intends this book to be a definitive study on any of the topics it discusses. Instead, she hopes it will be the beginning of an unending, delightful journey along the highways and byways of the topics. And at the end of the journey, after we have all met with Jesus face-to-face, she is looking forward to hearing many more of your wonderful stories of God's love and grace.

INTRODUCTION

This book is a celebration of stories. Stories Christ told. And stories some of you have told.

Christ's stories teach us about the Christian journey. They are signposts that direct us along a path to a good place—the foot of the cross, where we listen to the greatest story ever told. This good place is common ground for all Christians, despite age, gender, or nationality. And this good place is the right place to tell and to hear one another's stories. Stories we have grown up with and in. Stories that reflect what occurred in the parables—things that happened because of the greatest story.

We are meant to take courage for the journey from both Christ's stories and our stories. The stories keep our hope and faith alive. So, come. Gather 'round. There are stories to tell. There are stories to hear. Stories of Christ's love and grace.

That reminds me of a story. . . .

Chapter 1

GRACE NOTES

The parable

"It's gone!" Debra shrieked.

"What's gone?" Dave queried as he rushed into the dining room where his wife began scattering the contents of her purse across the table.

"My credit-card wallet! It's gone! Let's see. Where did I use it last? Hmmm. It was at the dry cleaners. I came back to the car, put the clothes in the back seat . . . Oh no! I put the wallet on top of the car so I could unlock the door, forgot about it, then drove off with it still there!"

"You retrace the route you drove home, and I'll stay here in case someone finds it and tries to call," Dave suggested. "Stop at the cleaners too. Maybe someone turned it in there."

All the way to the cleaners, all the way back, there was no sign of the missing valuable. On the return trip, Debra even stopped to check sewer drains. Then, just as she rounded the last corner before their house, she saw a black, square object lying in the weeds along the roadside. *What are the chances?* she wondered out loud. But she couldn't risk taking the chance that it *wasn't* the object of her search.

"Great news! I found it! I found it!" she exclaimed with joy, flinging open their front door.

"What a relief!" Dave embraced his wife as they skipped around the dining room, jubilant that the lost had been found.

How many times have we all nearly panicked just after real-

9

izing we had lost some common, yet valuable item. A set of keys. A checkbook. Or a computer disk with our latest work on it.

In Luke 15:4-7, Jesus tells a tale about an everyday object that was lost and rejoiced over when found. But while this story is about an ordinary object, it is not an ordinary story. Indeed, it portrays the very essence of the gospel. "For God so loved the world that He gave His only begotten Son, that whoever believes in Him should not perish but have everlasting life. For God did not send His Son into the world to condemn the world, but that the world through Him might be saved" (John 3:16, 17, NKJV).

We are valuable because God loves us, because He created us and redeems us. The lost lamb is the world, or more specifically, each of us individually, while the shepherd is God's Son, Jesus. And three particular aspects of the parable show us exactly how much God values us.

First of all, the parable opens with a dramatic search conducted by the shepherd upon learning one of his sheep is missing. This search is (1) a definite search; (2) an all-consuming search; (3) an active, personal search; and (4) a persistent search.

1. *A definite search.* When the shepherd realizes that one of the sheep is lost, he leaves the other sheep and looks specifically for that one. Might there be lost sheep from other flocks to confuse the shepherd? Yes and no. There might be lost sheep from other flocks. But they would not confuse the shepherd, for the relationship between a shepherd and his sheep is a close one. Sheep often remain with a flock for eight to nine years, long enough for the shepherd to name them (John 10:3) and for them to recognize their shepherd's own signature call (verses 3, 5). Furthermore, when the flock entered the fold at night, the shepherd held his rod across the entrance a few inches above ground. As each sheep passed under the rod, the shepherd inspected it for injuries and illness. Thus, the shepherd most likely could identify his own sheep rather quickly.

Likewise, while it is true that Jesus died to save humankind, He still calls us individually. (For example, see Matt. 9:9;

Luke 1:26, 27; Acts 9:1-6.) "The shepherd goes out to search for one sheep—the very least that can be numbered. So if there had been but one lost soul, Christ would have died for that one."—*Christ's Object Lessons*, 187.

2. *An all-consuming search.* Because he can think of nothing else, the shepherd leaves the rest of the flock to find the missing sheep. (The shepherd does not leave the ninety-nine in danger. The wilderness referred to is the unfarmed pasture lands, hills, and valleys where the sheep grazed.)

How like Christ, whose singleness of purpose is displayed in His willingness to leave heaven that He might save us. He, "being in very nature God, did not consider equality with God something to be grasped, but made himself nothing, taking the very nature of a servant, being made in human likeness. And being found in appearance as a man, he humbled himself and became obedient to death—even death on a cross!" (Phil. 2:6-8).

3. *An active, personal search.* The shepherd does not send someone else to do his work. He becomes personally involved. He knows the sheep so well, how could he do otherwise?

So it is with Christ. Because He created us, He knows us better than anyone. He does not, He cannot send another to do His work. Only He can redeem us. "The Sovereign Lord says: *I myself* will search for my sheep and look after them. . . . *I* will rescue them from all the places where they were scattered on a day of clouds and darkness" (Ezek. 34:11, 12, emphasis supplied).

4. *A persistent search.* The shepherd did not stop searching until he found the sheep. Likewise, Jesus searches for us until He finds us. Hopefully, we, like the sheep, will allow Him to carry us home.

Just as the shepherd's search indicates how much God values us, so does the behavior of the shepherd, once he finds the sheep. He does not chide it for nibbling itself away from the flock, nor does he drive it or lead it back. Instead, he *lifts* it to his shoulders, where it stays until they return to the others. From this we learn that:

1. *We belong to Jesus. We are exclusively His.* Has the Lord lifted you from the entangling briars of sin? Do you depend on

Him alone to sustain you? "I give them eternal life, and they shall never perish; no one can snatch them out of my hand. My Father, who has given them to me, is greater than all; no one can snatch them out of my Father's hand" (John 10:28, 29).

2. *Jesus wishes to serve us.* Indeed, that was His purpose for becoming one with us. During the last Passover Jesus spent with His disciples, He told them in response to an argument they were having over which one of them was the greatest, that He was among them "as one who serves" (Luke 22:27). That service included bearing our sins upon the cross. Such a gesture, once comprehended even slightly, should put to rest all bickering.

3. *Jesus desires to give us rest.* What a relief when we finally understand that there is nothing we can do to earn salvation. "For it is by grace you have been saved, through faith—and this not from yourselves, it is the gift of God" (Eph. 2:8). "He saved us, not because of righteous things we had done, but because of his mercy. He saved us through the washing of rebirth and renewal by the Holy Spirit, whom he poured out on us generously through Jesus Christ our Savior" (Titus 3:5, 6).

"Let the beloved of the Lord rest secure in him, for he shields him all day long, and the one the Lord loves rests between his shoulders" (Deut. 33:12). Surefooted and strong, our Shepherd carries us back to safety. No part of the journey should frighten or worry us, for He holds us firmly.

The third aspect of the parable depicting how valuable we are to God is what happens when the shepherd returns home. The festive occasion he arranges symbolizes the joy in heaven when even just one sinner repents (Luke 15:6, 7). How incredible that after such an exhaustive search, that after carrying the sheep home on his shoulders, the shepherd does not simply deposit it with the rest of the flock, then slip away for some much-deserved rest.

How incredible that "Christ, the loved Commander in the heavenly courts, stooped from His high estate, laid aside the glory that He had with the Father, in order to save the one lost world. For this He left the sinless worlds on high, the ninety and nine that loved Him, and came to this earth, to be 'wounded for our transgressions' and 'bruised for our iniquities.' (Isa. 53:5.) God gave Himself in His Son that He might have the joy of receiving back the sheep that was lost."—*Christ's Object Lessons*, 190, 191.

Elsewhere in the Bible

Because the story of the lost sheep is the story of the gospel, the lives of many people in Scripture mirror the parable. And we need not look deep between the covers of the Bible to find the first such lives. When Adam and Eve chose to listen to Satan rather than their Creator, they essentially became lost sheep. Their choice separated them from God, rendering them helpless.

But God came looking for them. When Adam and Eve heard Him in the garden, they hid. But God was not deterred. As the shepherd in the parable, His search was definite, all-consuming, active, personal, and persistent. So He called to them, "Where are you?" (Gen. 3:9). And after He found them, He lifted them upon His shoulders by telling them how He planned to redeem them from their poor choice. "I will put enmity between you and the woman, and between your offspring and hers; he will crush your head, and you will strike his heel" (verse 15). The Christian church has always understood that this pronouncement foretells the incarnation of Christ. What stunning news it must have been for Adam and Eve to realize that "the value that God places on the work of His hands, the love He has for His children, is revealed by the gift He made to redeem men. Adam fell under the dominion of Satan. He brought sin into the world, and death by sin. God gave His only-begotten Son to save man. This He did that He might be just, and yet the justifier of all who accept Christ. Man sold himself to Satan, but Jesus bought back the race."—*Messages to Young People*, 69.

Your story

The value God places on us all still amazes people today. "Value," writes a woman named Grace, "is in the eye of the beholder. Fortunately for the human race, God's love sees each of us as valuable.

"Around the late 1930s, in one of New York City's ghettos, lived a teenager in whom God saw value. Despite being poor, female, and a member of a minority, God envisioned where I could be a willing and capable worker for Him. He saw value in me, which I would eventually appreciate. Already He had saved me from being abducted when I was ten.

"I was the oldest of seven children. Neither of my parents had attended school beyond the third grade. Conditions in our tenement apartment were crowded. Yet it seemed there was always room for one more child every other year or an adult needing help until he or she could accumulate enough resources to become self-sufficient. The higher people had to climb to get to their apartment, the lower their rent. The first floor was one flight up from the ground floor. So if people lived on the fourth floor, they climbed four flights. An apartment with five flights had an elevator. It wasn't until I was eighteen that I ever lived in any but a fourth-floor apartment.

"Therefore, I had two means of developing my lungs—climbing to the fourth floor or calling to my mother from the sidewalk! Calling was my preferred method in warm weather!

" 'Ma! Throw me a penny for some candy!' 'Ma! Can I get in the shower?' (During the summer months, the firemen would open the hydrants and create a shower effect by placing a barrel over the water spray.)

"Other good times consisted of going to the beach and to church with some of my neighbors. One day, Sister Gloria invited me to attend her Seventh-day Adventist church. Soon, Gloria's daughter and I became such good friends people referred to us as David and Jonathan. The church became my second mother and father. Though I was the only Adventist in my family for twenty years, I found warmth and fellowship among the other members and most assuredly in Sister Gloria's apartment just half a block away.

"It wasn't long after my baptism that I learned about the church's system of education. I could not afford to attend academy. But I soon learned that I could enroll in an Adventist college if I was willing to take my time and work hard. Much help, financial and otherwise, often came unsolicited. How thrilled I was when God took care of my needs through His own means. Eventually, He led me to a teaching position that placed me, the ghetto kid, before children from affluent, professional homes.

"One day, while I was reading the following scripture, I was stunned by the realization that I was special to God, that it didn't matter to Him if I was poor, female, and a member of a minority: 'There is neither Jew nor Greek, slave nor free, male nor female, for you are all one in Christ Jesus. If you belong to Christ, then you are Abraham's seed, and heirs according to the promise' (Gal. 3:28, 29). What really mattered? I was God's child. And He valued me—*Grace!*"

Now what?

The parable of the lost sheep is an appeal from God for us to repent. Through the figures of a helpless sheep and a determined, compassionate shepherd, we learn that "He reveals to us His love in order that we may repent."—*Christ's Object Lessons*, 189.

Why is repenting so important? It is the first step you must take toward salvation and your spiritual growth (Acts 2:37, 38; 3:19).

What does it mean to repent? The Hebrew word means "to be sorry," while the Greek word means "to change one's mind," "to feel remorse." Thus, to repent sincerely means to change completely your view of God and sin. This change occurs when you:

1. *sense*, through the promptings of the Holy Spirit, God's holiness and your sinfulness and lost condition;

2. *experience* sorrow and guilt as a result of discerning God's holiness and your sinfulness;

3. *confess* specific sins once you understand that "he who covers his sins will not prosper, but whoever confesses and forsakes them will have mercy" (Prov. 28:13, NKJV);

4. *surrender* completely to Christ; and

5. *renounce* your sinful actions through the exercise of your will and the assistance of the Holy Spirit.

These steps result in *conversion*, a turning away from sin

toward God (Acts 15:3).

Psalm 51 embodies the spirit of repentance. After having committed adultery and murder, David pleads:

> Have mercy upon me, O God,
>   According to Your lovingkindness;
> According to the multitude of Your
>   tender mercies,
> Blot out my transgressions. . . .
>
> For I acknowledge my transgressions,
> And my sin *is* ever before me.
> Against You, You only, have I sinned. . . .
>
> Make me to hear joy and gladness. . . .
>
> Create in me a clean heart, O God,
> And renew a steadfast spirit within me. . . .
>
> Restore to me the joy of Your salvation.
>   (verses 1-4, 8, 10, 12, NKJV).

David, once a strong, valiant shepherd, now a perishing, lost lamb, prays to be lifted upon the shoulders of his Shepherd Saviour and carried home to the joy that awaits him. May his prayer be yours.

Chapter 2

BEARING THE CROSS

The parables

Two or three building blocks plus a dozen or so stringing beads—the wood nicked, the paint chipped and peeling. An Uncle Wiggily book—its pages water-stained and frayed. A tin beach pail portraying carefree children sculpting sandcastles at the seashore—a tad rusty from the water's edge.

But wait. What was this fur?

I can't believe it! Ted nearly exclaimed as he stopped rummaging through the box of old toys, the auction crowd milling around him. There lay a five-inch-long Shuco teddy bear constructed of golden mohair and glass eyes. He sported a red ribbon around his neck and extending from his side a wind-up key that when taut, caused him to somersault. Cautiously holding the bear out of sight, Ted turned the key. When the tiny bruin tumbled head-over-heels, Ted could hardly contain himself. Off he scurried to find his wife, Barb, inform her of his discovery, and discuss with her what their bid should be for the container of trinkets, one of which was a legitimate treasure.

As antique toy collectors, Ted and Barb knew the value of their discovery—approximately six-hundred fifty dollars!—and were willing to pay the price necessary to obtain it. They also were quite certain from observing the interests of other bargain hunters that toys would not be hot items. Even the auction house had proven it was not aware of the bear's value by tossing it in a container they would auction as a unit.

17

Jesus told several parables that deal with the value of a treasure—*that* treasure being His kingdom. These parables are found in Matthew 13:44-46, Luke 12:13-34, and 14:25-35. They cause us to search our hearts by asking, Do I recognize the value of the kingdom of heaven? What will God's kingdom cost me personally? Am I willing to pay that price?

Two of these stories Jesus told while He was traveling to Jerusalem for the last time (Luke 14:28-32). The crowds milling around Him were hoping that before long He would revolt against Roman oppression by proclaiming Himself leader of Israel. But Jesus knew that instead of delighting in a coronation, they soon would be demanding a crucifixion.

Thus He turned to them and warned, "Anyone who does not carry his cross and follow me cannot be my disciple" (Luke 14:27). The two parables follow this warning and serve to emphasize the point He wants His would-be disciples to understand, "Before you decide to follow Me, you must know the cost of doing so and decide if you are willing to pay it. For the price of being My disciple will be to endure your own cross."

How odd! Wasn't the cross an instrument of capital punishment reserved only for slaves, the worst criminals, and non-Romans? Didn't Hebrew law pronounce a curse upon anyone who was crucified (Deut. 21:23; Gal. 3:13)? Weren't victims flogged prior to crucifixion, then forced to carry their cross, or at least the crossbeam, to the place of execution, where they would linger at death's border for hours, quite possibly days? Truly, to die on a cross was to die in humiliation.

But that humiliation is just the point. Arrogant people believe they know everything, can do everything, and are in need of no one and nothing. They boast of their riches, their acquired wealth, and the "fact" that they lack nothing (Rev. 3:17). Because crosses require voluntary self-denial on a daily basis (Luke 9:23), they are impediments that comfortable, proud people choose to avoid. Their lives are so full of the trappings of pride there is no room for Christ, who describes Himself as "meek and lowly in heart" (Matt. 11:29, KJV).

The Greek word translated "meek," however, does not mean to be ineffectual, powerless, or cowardly. Rather, it means "to be tamed." It characterizes a person who possesses self-control and self-discipline. Those who are meek are truly humble. Pride equals self-sufficiency, while meekness equals submitting to God and His will.

To live in submission to God and His will is to take up your cross. And to take up your cross is to die to (1) the world's set of values and (2) to self.

1. *Dying to the world's set of values.* The world measures value by the material goods people possess or by the amount of power they are able to flaunt. Christianity assesses value according to the amount people give away (Mark 12:41-44) and the service they provide (Acts 9:36-42; Matt. 25:31-46). When you take up your cross, you sacrifice your desire to own all the latest gadgets and the urge always to be in control.

> The cross means sharing the suffering of Christ to the last and to the fullest. . . . The first Christ-suffering which every man must experience is the call to abandon the attachments of this world. It is that dying of the old man which is the result of his encounter with Christ. As we embark upon discipleship we surrender ourselves to Christ in union with his death—we give over our lives to death. Thus it begins; the cross is not the terrible end to an otherwise godfearing and happy life, but it meets us at the beginning of our communion with Christ.—Dietrich Bonhoeffer, *The Cost of Discipleship* (New York: Macmillan Publishing Co., 1975), 98, 99.

2. *Dying to self.* When you take up your cross to follow Christ, you can no longer please yourself. You place yourself completely within the boundaries of His biddings. On your cross, you sacrifice your personal aspirations: the career you might have attained; the prosperity and comfort you might have enjoyed; in short, you sacrifice your own will and desires.

> To deny oneself is to be aware only of Christ and no more of self, to see only him who goes before and no more the road which is too hard for us. Once more, all

that self-denial can say is: "He leads the way, keep close to him."

Only when we have become completely oblivious of self are we ready to bear the cross for his sake. If in the end we know only him, if we have ceased to notice the pain of our own cross, we are indeed looking only unto him.—Bonhoeffer, 97.

In addition to these two general aspects of cross-bearing is the truth that each dedicated Christian will be asked to bear a cross specific only to him or her. Albert Schweitzer chose to bear the cross of Lambarene. Mother Teresa chose to bear Calcutta, and George Washington Carver the education of African Americans after the United States Civil War. Ellen White's cross was the establishment and nurture of the Seventh-day Adventist Church, while Amanda Smith, once a slave in the United States, chose the cross of missionary evangelist, preaching in England, India, Africa, and other parts of the world.

Our cross is that difficult thing we choose to do because we are His people. . . . We choose a hard place, a difficult relationship, a thankless job. We serve on a committee, or get involved with a neighbor. We do the things we don't have to do because we feel it is God's agenda for us. We say, like Isaiah, " 'Here am I. Send me.' "—Bruce Larson, *The Communicator's Commentary—Luke*, Lloyd J. Ogilvie, General Editor (Waco, Tex.: Word Books, 1983), 171.

We are not to confuse our cross with the thorns of life. One year, Rob and Beth suffered from the sharp jabs of illness plus financial setbacks. But as burdensome as this was, it was not a cross, for it was not chosen. We choose to carry our crosses, to be a member of that tedious committee or to continue pursuing that difficult relationship with a person who always seems to need our help.

Christ came to heal the wounds that thorns inflict. And

we can be burden-bearers with each other in our suffering. But suffering in itself is not noble. It is simply part of life. When you are able to endure a painful thorn in the flesh by the grace of God, you are a profound witness to your contemporaries. . . .

God's grace is seen in His people in the way we carry our thorns and survive, not somehow, but triumphantly. But God wants to share His glory with us, and that happens when we pick up our cross. —Larson, 170, 171.

Elsewhere in the Bible

Who in Scripture chose to pick up their cross? And what price did they pay to gain the treasure of the kingdom of heaven? Perhaps one of the most famous cross-bearers is Noah, who sacrificed a respectable place in his community to carry his cross—a cross that came in the shape of a boat 450 feet long, 75 wide, and 45 feet high! This vessel was to harbor him and his family from a flood that would destroy the world and the wickedness in it. But if that wasn't enough, he agreed "to preach that God would bring a flood of water upon the earth to destroy the wicked. Those who would believe the message, and would prepare for that event by repentance and reformation, should find pardon and be saved."—*Patriarchs and Prophets*, 92.

We can imagine how people must have lost respect for Noah when we realize that up until then rain had never fallen, a mist or dew watering the earth instead (*Patriarchs and Prophets*, 96, 97). How his friends and neighbors must have ridiculed him as he painstakingly gathered materials and began such a laborious project. "But Noah stood like a rock amid the tempest. Surrounded by popular contempt and ridicule, he distinguished himself by his holy integrity and unwavering faithfulness. A power attended his words, for it was the voice of God to man through His servant. Connection with God made him strong in the strength of infinite power, while for one hundred and twenty years his solemn voice fell upon the ears of that generation in regard to events, which, so far as human wisdom could judge, were impossible."—*Patriarchs and Prophets*, 96.

Another person whose words were filled with God's power was Deborah, the only one of Israel's judges who apparently also held the office of prophet. "After Ehud died, the Israelites once again did evil in the eyes of the Lord. So the Lord sold them into the hands of Jabin, a king of Canaan, who reigned in Hazor. The commander of his army was Sisera, who lived in Harosheth Haggoyim. Because he had nine hundred iron chariots and had cruelly oppressed the Israelites for twenty years, they cried to the Lord for help" (Judges 4:1-3). And Deborah was the person God called upon to assist Him.

As she held court each day under a palm tree between Ramah and Bethel, Deborah displayed qualities of common sense and wisdom. And as a prophet, it is likely she spent time recalling for her people their history in Egypt and Sinai and prophesying of better days to come. Thus they felt confident rallying around her when she called Barak to lead a mere 10,000 men against Jabin's 900 iron chariots.

When Sisera heard that the Israelites had gathered on Mt. Tabor, he advanced his chariots to the Kishon River, where unknown to him, the Lord had promised Deborah to defeat him (Judges 4:7). Upon receiving word from God through Deborah, Barak and his army descended the mountain. Then "the Lord routed Sisera and all his chariots and army by the sword, and Sisera abandoned his chariot and fled on foot. . . . All the troops of Sisera fell by the sword; not a man was left" (verses 15, 16).

How was Deborah able to carry her cross as judge and prophet? She tells us herself when she asks Barak, "Has not the Lord gone ahead of you?" (verse 14). Thus she was able to sing, "March on, my soul, be strong!" (5:21).

Pondering the lives of these two cross-bearers tells us that the cost of following Jesus may involve:

1. Doing the unusual, the unheard of, or even the impossible
2. Losing friends and gaining enemies
3. Leaving the comfort of home
4. Working with stubborn people (Judg. 4:8)
5. Engaging in arduous daily tasks

But hasn't the Lord gone ahead of us? Is there anything in

the above list He has not done? Then march on! Be strong! He already has carried His cross. He already has paid the price.

Your story

With these words Sharon begins telling how she exchanged earthly treasures for a cross:

"As a teenager, trusting Jesus brought me much joy. But the man I married when I was twenty-one years old claimed to be an atheist. Gradually I stopped going to church, praying, and reading my Bible. For twenty-three years, I ignored God.

"When my husband became mentally imbalanced, he resigned his position on the staff of a medical school. Soon my children and I were penniless. After three years of working several jobs at once, as well as taking college courses, I was hired to be the administrative assistant to the dean of medicine at the University of Texas Medical Branch, in Galveston. I started dating one of the most eligible bachelors in town. My son was a junior in college, and my daughter was in junior high school.

"But despite this success, I still felt empty. Then something else happened that changed our lives again. One day I was washing dishes in my apartment when suddenly a thought came to me from nowhere, *There isn't much time*. I dismissed it immediately. Often, however, I would be at work, grocery shopping, or on a date when this same thought would reoccur. It would loom in my mind—hard, low, and firm. *There isn't much time*.

"Finally, I decided this must be a premonition that I was going to die. So that my children would be cared for, I proceeded to settle my affairs. I also began to stay home on Saturday nights, reading my Bible and praying. I began to miss the close walk with Jesus I had as a teenager. Gradually, I realized I must give up all I had worked so hard for in order to really surrender my life to Him. My mind warred with itself. I was quite reluctant to give up a secure, good-paying job. I really enjoyed my many friends. Because my son was in his senior year of college, I kept praying, 'Lord, as soon as he graduates, I'll turn my life over to You. I just can't afford to let him down now.'

"But there was a tugging at my heart to sell all I had, to

trust in Jesus to care for my children. So I finally surrendered. I gave three months' notice to my employer and began to sell my furniture and jewelry to gather cash for my new adventure. An answer to prayer came from a friend who offered me a place to stay for three months in a mobile home on a beautiful lake. Also, he said if I would pay for the needed repairs on his second car, I could use it. God was opening doors one step at a time— one day at a time.

"It was difficult for about two years, and I was tested severely. But I have never regretted this move. I was able to live my life just as I thought Jesus wanted me to, and I was introduced to the Seventh-day Adventist Church. Both my children became Christians and were baptized. My son graduated from college; I found two good jobs; and I was able to buy a new three-bedroom, two-bath home on a wooded lot.

"Thus, I ended up with more than I had originally. Plus my children and I had the peace and joy that Christ brings. Five years later, God again asked me to sell everything and move, teaching me that one-time surrender isn't enough. He asks us to take up our cross *daily* and follow Him. Earthly treasures never can take the place of the joy and peace we have when we submit to His will. Now I know that *There isn't enough time* means Jesus is returning soon, and we should live our lives not in accumulating security and wealth on this earth, but in building up treasures in heaven."

Now what?

Picking up your cross and carrying it is possible only if you maintain a strong connection with God and you are not carrying anything else. Unfortunately, the rich fool in Luke 12:13-21 didn't realize this. How much he is like the people described in Revelation 3:17! One would think *he* had caused the rain to fall, the sun to shine, and the seed to sprout! His hands were so full of his abundant crop, he wouldn't have been able to pick up his cross if it had been made of gold!

Then there was the rich, young ruler who was so preoccupied with his "great possessions" that when presented with his cross, he turned from Jesus, sorrowing that he could not hold on to both his wealth and his Saviour (Matt. 19:16-22).

Why could this ruler not have kept his riches? Because he valued them more than he valued Jesus. Upon counting the cost of following Jesus, he discovered that he could not pay the price. Boasting, he replied to Christ that he was quite adept at obeying the commandments, including the directive to love his neighbor as himself. But he condemns himself as he weaves his way back through the crowd. If he really had loved his neighbors as himself, he would not have hesitated to share his possessions with them. He was so proud of his commandment-keeping abilities. But he had just broken another one—"You shall have no other gods before me" (Exod. 20:3). The issue is not whether it is lawful for a Christian to have possessions or substantial investment portfolios. Rather, the issue is, Are such objects of more value than Christ?

How can you make sure that, unlike these two foolish rich men, your hands are free to accept your cross? One way is to live a life of simplicity.

But how can you do that? By living to seek first the kingdom of God and His righteousness (Matt. 6:33). It is really a matter of priorities. What you value most will determine what choice you make when Christ presents you with your cross.

Seeking God's kingdom above all else will affect your lifestyle. Such a lifestyle will take on as many different forms as there are Christians. But following are five principles that can help all of us empty our hands so we will be able to pick up our cross and follow Jesus.[1]

1. *Purchase items for their usefulness instead of their status.* For example, you commute quite a distance to work, so you need a comfortable car that gets good gas mileage, not the hot little sports number many people are acquiring despite the fact it rated poorly in crash tests.

2. *Avoid gadgets that claim they will make your life easier.* Does the new refrigerator you need really have to have an ice-making machine and a water dispenser?

3. *Avoid "buy now, pay later" plans.* Brian and Mary bought some family-room furniture this way. A year later, when the bill came due, they realized they had forgotten about it. Their

furniture was repossessed.

4. *Cultivate a deeper appreciation for creation.* Watch the stars come out in the evening. Plant flowers and shrubs that attract birds and butterflies. Go for walks and notice how many colors, textures, and patterns exist in just your neighborhood. As you notice this variety, consider how creative God is. Soon nature will be your entertainment.

5. *Use plain, honest speech* (see Ps. 34:13). Avoid exaggeration, jargon, flattery, gossip, and half-truths. Speak less; listen more. And if you agree to do something, do it.

Perhaps Solomon's thoughts on simplicity say it best: "I denied myself nothing my eyes desired; I refused my heart no pleasure. . . . Yet when I surveyed all that my hands had done . . . everything was meaningless. . . . [Only] God gives wisdom, knowledge and happiness" (Eccl. 2:10, 11, 26).

What price are you willing to pay to bear your cross?

---

1. These principles are adapted from Richard J. Foster, *Celebration of Discipline: The Path to Spiritual Growth*, rev. ed. (New York, N.Y.: Harper Collins Publishers, 1988), 90-95.

Chapter 3

SAFE IN THE ARMS

The parable

If you've never been stressed out about something, then you're not human. But how we react to stress and tension can make a huge difference in our quality of life. One of the most widely reported studies showing that chronic stress can lead to a depressed immune system involved sixty-nine people who, for at least five years, had been the primary care givers for their spouses suffering from Alzheimer's Disease. When compared to a similar group of noncare-giving adults, the care givers showed decreases in three measures of cellular immunity. They also had been sick for more days with respiratory-tract infections. Furthermore, care givers who were worried the most by the dementia-related behavior of their loved ones and who experienced lower levels of social support encountered the greatest decline in immunity.

Jesus cautions us against the effects of worry on our spiritual health in the parable of the sower (Matt. 13:1-9, 18-23). In this story, three types of soil symbolize different people and what happens to them after they accept the gospel message.

The good soil represents people who accept Christ, obey Him, and grow the fruit of the Spirit—a Christlike character. The stony soil represents people who accept Christ with joy but then neglect to count the cost of following Him. Thus, when temptation and suffering beat upon them like stones, they retreat to their comfortable former life. The thorny soil represents people who experience the new birth but fail to mature, the prickly worries of life stunting their growth. It is this soil in which many of us are rooted.

But what exactly is worry? The word itself comes from an ancient Anglo-Saxon word that means to strangle or to choke. A. S. Roche believes that "worry is a thin stream of fear trickling through the mind. If encouraged, it cuts a channel into which all other thoughts are drained." And E. Stanley Jones states that "worry is sin against the loving care of the Father." This last definition becomes even more meaningful when we take time to consider Jesus' words in Matthew 6:25-34. When worries, like enemy soldiers, threaten to pillage our faith and trust in God, Jesus would like us to remember that the birds work hard to eat. But unlike the rich fool (Luke 12:13-34), they do not worry or strain to insure that in five years "down the road" or ten, they will have a storehouse of plenty. The heavenly Father takes care of them. And are you not more valuable than they?

Then there are the flowers to consider. Perhaps as Jesus spoke, He and His listeners could gaze upon the poppies and anemones swaying in the breeze. They blossomed for only a day. And when they withered, Palestinian women burned them in their boxy clay ovens to quickly raise the temperature. "Yet I tell you that not even Solomon in all his splendor was dressed like one of these. If that is how God clothes the grass of the field, which is here today and tomorrow is thrown into the fire, will he not much more clothe you?" (Matt. 6:29, 30).

Jesus also would like us to remember that worry is: (1) injurious, (2) irreverent, (3) irrelevant, and (4) irresponsible.

1. *Worry is injurious.* We have already established in the beginning of this chapter that worrying can cause physical health problems. And, of course, it can seriously damage our spiritual health. Is there a greater sin than worry? Surely we could debate this. But surely, there is no more paralyzing sin than worry. When we focus on our concerns, we prevent ourselves from growing in God's love and grace, and from dealing justly with the true concerns of others (Luke 12:22, 32-34).

2. *Worry is irreverent.* It is a lack of faith in the God who

gives us life and sustains it (Matt. 6:30). Such a lack is under-standable if a person believes God is fickle and impulsive. But such a lack from someone who calls God Father is unintelligible.

3. *Worry is irrelevant*. We cannot change a situation by fretting about it. Nor does doing so help us cope more efficiently. "And can any of you by worrying add a single hour to your span of life?" (Matt. 6:27, NRSV). (As evidenced by medical research, worry may even shorten your life!)

4. *Worry is irresponsible*. When we spend time fussing and fuming about our problems, we squander energy we could use more productively. "Worry is utterly useless. It never serves a good purpose. It brings no good results. One cannot think or see clearly when worrying."—Corrie Ten Boom, *Don't Wrestle, Just Nestle* (Old Tappan, N.J.: Fleming H. Revell Company, 1978), 36.

We can trace much of what we worry about back to our attempts at trying to serve two masters—mammon (an Aramaic word referring to wealth, profit, property, and, quite possibly, treasure) and God. That Jesus was well aware of such attempts is evident in Matthew 6:19-24 where He gives us three short but succinct proverbs.

1. *Verses 19-21*. Here Jesus warns us that earthly treasures will decay, leaving us with nothing. Moths will destroy in storage the elaborate garments composing much of a man's wealth (2 Kings 5:22; Josh. 7:21). Grain that is stored for too long a time will fall prey to gnawing worms and rats.[1] And anything of value, such as a small container of gold stored in one's house, would be an easy target for thieves who were willing and able to "break through" (KJV) the usual weak, clay walls.

Jesus' advice to concentrate on eternal treasures is just as forceful today as we witness earthly possessions being destroyed by earthquakes, fires, hurricanes, monsoons, tornadoes, floods, etc.

2. *Verses 22, 23*. It is difficult, if not impossible, for the eye to focus on two different things at once. So it is with people who, like the rich young ruler (Matt. 19:16-22), attempt to devote themselves to gaining both the treasures of

this world and God's kingdom. But

> a Christian whose spiritual "eye" is "single," . . . is one whose insight and judgment make him a man of unaffected simplicity, artless, plain, and pure. He sees the things of time and eternity in true perspective.
>
> Singleness of eyesight results in singleness of purpose, in wholehearted devotion to the kingdom of heaven and to the practice of its eternal principles (Phil. 3:8, 13, 14 . . .). To be effective, vision must be focused and concentrated. In the same way, the man who desires true light in his soul must have his spiritual eyesight in sharp focus. Otherwise his vision will be blurred and his estimation of truth and duty will be faulty.—*SDA Bible Commentary*, 5: 350.

3. *Verse 24*. Just as the eye cannot focus clearly on two objects at the same time, so two opposing forces cannot control the heart at the same time. In this instance, the two opposing forces are God and mammon. Jesus is not saying that wealth in itself is wrong but that our selfish devotion to it is. "The love of money is the root of all evil" (1 Tim. 6:10, KJV; see also James 5:1-6).

> We cannot serve God with a divided heart. Bible religion is not one influence among many others; its influence is to be supreme, pervading and controlling every other. It is not to be like a dash of color brushed here and there upon the canvas, but it is to pervade the whole life, as if the canvas were dipped into the color, until every thread of the fabric were dyed a deep, unfading hue. . . .
>
> Worldly policy and the undeviating principles of righteousness do not blend into each other imperceptibly, like the colors of the rainbow. Between the two a broad, clear line is drawn by the eternal God. The likeness of Christ stands out as distinct from that of Satan as midday in contrast with midnight. . . . If

one sin is cherished in the soul, or one wrong practice
retained in the life, the whole being is contaminated.
—*The Desire of Ages*, 312, 313.

What are the treasures of heaven of which worry can rob us?
Earlier, this chapter stated that the good soil in the parable of
the sower represents people who accept Christ, obey Him, and
grow the fruit of the Spirit, while the thorny soil symbolizes
people who experience the new birth but fail to grow mature
fruit because worry impedes their development. "The fruit of
the Spirit is love, joy, peace, patience, kindness, goodness, faithfulness, gentleness and self-control" (Gal. 5:22, 23). These treasures describe: (1) the character of Christ (His righteousness;
see Exod. 33:18, 19) and (2) the life we are to live by the Spirit
(verse 19), the two being treasures in themselves. That Jesus
was willing to save us and renew His image in us (the gospel)
is yet another heavenly treasure equal to any other.

God desires us to choose the heavenly in place of the
earthly. He opens before us the possibilities of a
heavenly investment. He would give encouragement to
our loftiest aims, security to our choicest treasure. He
declares, "I will make a man more precious than fine
gold; even a man than the golden wedge of Ophir." Isa.
13:12. When the riches that moth devours and rust
corrupts shall be swept away, Christ's followers can
rejoice in their heavenly treasure, the riches that are
imperishable. —*Christ's Object Lessons*, 374.

Elsewhere in the Bible

Anyone who has hosted a meal, particularly when a special
friend or important person is in attendance, can sympathize
with Martha. You're scrambling around, worrying about every
detail, while everyone else is enjoying the honored guest! But
it is this very scenario that Christ used to help us better understand that worry separates us from Him.

Having no home of His own, Christ must have appreciated
the opportunity to visit with His friends, Mary, Martha, and

Lazarus. In their home, He could escape the crowds, who mostly misunderstood His message, and the Pharisees, who dogged His steps everywhere He went. During this particular visit, Martha was frantic with worry over the dinner preparations, while Mary "sat at the Lord's feet listening to what he said" (Luke 10:39). Thus, Martha pleads with her Saviour, "Lord, don't you care that my sister has left me to do the work by myself? Tell her to help me!" (Luke 10:40). But it was this very attitude Jesus cautioned against in Matthew 6:25-34. And His answer to Martha rings with that same caution, "Martha, Martha, . . . you are worried and upset about many things, but only one thing is needed. Mary has chosen what is better and it will not be taken away from her" (Luke 10:41, 42).

With her heart undivided, Mary was able to focus her attention on Jesus, "storing her mind with the precious words falling from the Saviour's lips, words that were more precious to her than earth's most costly jewels."

> The "one thing" that Martha needed was a calm, devotional spirit, a deeper anxiety for knowledge concerning the future, immortal life, and the graces necessary for spiritual advancement. She needed less anxiety for the things which pass away, and more for those things which endure forever. Jesus would teach His children to seize every opportunity of gaining that knowledge which will make them wise unto salvation. The cause of Christ needs careful, energetic workers. There is a wide field for the Marthas, with their zeal in active religious work. But let them first sit with Mary at the feet of Jesus. Let diligence, promptness, and energy be sanctified by the grace of Christ; then the life will be an unconquerable power for good.—*The Desire of Ages*, 525.

Later in Scripture, Mary kneels once again at the feet of Jesus, this time to wipe them with her hair, her tears, and an ointment which most likely cost a year's wages (300 denarii; John 12:1-8). Judas thought her behavior extravagant, even sinful. " 'Why wasn't this perfume sold and the money given to the poor?' . . . [But] he did not say this because he cared about the poor but because he was thief; as keeper of the money bag, he used to help himself to what was put into it" (verse 6). A short time later, he would betray Christ for a paltry thirty pieces of silver, the price of a slave!

Christ's desire to be present in our lives, to fellowship with us, is as sincere today as it was when He lived on earth. And our need for "a calm, devotional spirit," coupled with a deep appreciation for heavenly wealth, is as great today as it was when Mary placed her cares in His keeping. Exactly what *are* our worries worth? What will *you* trade them for?

Your story

"I sighed a worried sigh as I leaned back in the rocking chair, my head pressing against its pillowed back," Lori writes of a time well remembered.

"*Oh, Lord.* The prayer formed only in my mind, not wishing to wake the infant I held. *Are You listening?* A tear dripped from my chin onto my son's head. But the little boy nestled his head against my shoulder, such a peaceful expression on his face.

"*Lord, You know he's only two months old, that I love him so much. But he's up twice a night to be fed, and I'm so tired.* I thought about all the baby books I'd read before his birth. The big advice was rest when the baby is sleeping. Except, what do working mothers do?

"*Dear Jesus, You know I truly believe You want me to teach this year. But this baby came so late I only had a week to get ready for classes. Lord, I'm so tired. I can't keep up with all the dirty diapers.* The tears fell faster. *School always wears me out the first few weeks. But never have I felt like this. Help me! Please help me!*

"The baby stirred again, sighing peacefully. *Oh, Lord, this little fella has such trust in his daddy and me. We don't want to let him down. But I don't know if I can keep going. I wish I could snuggle up against You, Lord, and sleep soundly in Your arms the way he does in mine. I wish I didn't have to worry about tomorrow.*

"Then it came to me. A picture of myself leaning *my* head against God's chest, His arms wrapped protectively around *me*. The baby and I both breathed deeply. The Father kissed *my* furrowed forehead as I had kissed the baby's so many times before. And with one hand, He stroked *my* back to relieve the stressed muscles. Finally I felt I could face the trials of another day, knowing I could rest safely in my heavenly Father's arms. *Thank You, Jesus, for showing me You haven't left me. Thank You for giving me the strength to keep doing Your will.*

"It has been more than nine years since that little boy felt his mother's hot tears of exhaustion splash on his perfect skin. That night, I reached an all-time low. But God heard my inaudible cry for help and answered it in a tangible way for me. The peace I felt that night has continued to be with me through the birth of another precious son and a nonstop career as an elementary school teacher. And now, whenever I feel the thorns of worry beginning to prick, I reflect once again on being sheltered in God's loving arms."

Now what?

Lori discovered that such reflection, or meditation, helped her to cultivate the thorny soil of her heart, making it more fertile for spiritual growth.

> The Bible uses two different Hebrew words . . . to convey the idea of meditation, and together they are used some fifty-eight times. These words have various meanings: listening to God's word, reflecting on God's works, rehearsing God's deeds, ruminating on God's law, and more. In each case there is stress upon changed behavior as a result of our encounter with the living God.—Richard J. Foster, *Celebration of Discipline: The Path to Spiritual Growth*, rev. ed. (New York, N.Y.: HarperCollins Publishers, 1988), 15.

Moses counseled Israel to meditate on God's commandments at all times, in all places (Deut. 6:4-9). And God advised Joshua at the beginning of his career to meditate on the book of the Law (Josh. 1:8). The psalmist tells us that people who do so are blessed (Ps. 1:1, 2).Jesus Himself was aware of the blessings of meditation. Early in the morning, He often would retreat to a secluded spot to commune with His Father (Mark 1:35). And He would invite His disciples to go with Him "to a quiet place and get some rest" (Mark 6:31), knowing that "all who are under the training of God need the quiet hour for communion with their own hearts, with nature, and with God. . . . We must individually hear Him speaking to the heart. When every other voice is hushed, and in quietness we wait before Him, the silence of the soul makes more distinct the voice of God. He bids us, 'Be still, and know that I am God.' Psalm 46:10."—*The Ministry of Healing*, 58.

In addition to what already has been mentioned, what else can we reflect upon during the quiet hours of meditation?

1. "That we are in God's world, in the presence of the Creator; that we are made in His likeness; that He watches over us and loves us and cares for us—these are wonderful themes for thought and lead the mind into broad, exalted fields of meditation."—*Child Guidance*, 509.

2. "Recreation in the open air, the contemplation of the works of God in nature, will be of the highest benefit."—*The Adventist Home*, 496.

3. "It would be well to spend a thoughtful hour each day reviewing the life of Christ from the manger to Calvary. We should take it point by point and let the imagination vividly grasp each scene, especially the closing ones of His earthly life. By thus contemplating His teachings and sufferings, and the infinite sacrifice made by Him for the redemption of the race, we may strengthen our faith, quicken our love, and become more deeply imbued with the spirit which sustained our Saviour."—*Testimonies for the Church*, 4:374.

Thus your life will be redirected so you can deal more successfully with your problems. As the voice of God becomes more distinct, speaking to your heart alone, the thorns in your soil will wither, your worries will take flight.

---

1. The word translated *rust* (verse 20) means "to eat" or "to gnaw" and is translated as *rust* only in this passage. Thus it is quite possible Jesus is referring to the destruction by pests of stored crops. Fine clothing, abundant crops, and small amounts of gold or silver stored in a man's home often constituted the three main sources of wealth in Palestine at that time.

Chapter 4

SKELETON SOLDIERS

The parable

Have you ever huddled around a campfire on a dark night, telling and listening to scary stories? Jesus' parable of the haunted house in Matthew 12:43-45 would have been a good one for such an occasion. Surely some of His listeners must have related well to it because of the commonly held belief that empty houses supposedly were inhabited by evil spirits.

What did this strange parable mean? First of all, evil can be driven away but not exterminated like termites or ants. Because of its very nature, it will always be searching for ways to recover the ground it lost.

Second, a religion that frees people of evil but does not replace that evil with goodness is nothing more than a list of strict dos and don'ts and, as such, is a religion doomed to failure. Such a religion can free people from evil for a time. But it cannot keep them free unless the evil is replaced with something good. It is not enough simply to despise what is bad. We must embrace what is positive.

Suppose a man enters into possession of a garden which has run wild. He digs it, takes out the weeds and cleanses the whole place. But if he leaves it like that the weeds will come back and cover the soil again. He cannot leave it empty; he must go on to plant flowers; and in the end he must plant so many flowers that there is no room for weeds.—William Barclay, *And Jesus Said: A Handbook on the Parables of Jesus* (Philadelphia: The Westminster Press, 1970), 196.

But how are we to go about embracing the good so the evil will not return once it has been expelled? Part of the answer is, we ourselves cannot. When we *do* try, the result is that that list of dos and don'ts, and the failure to keep such a list, becomes all too personal and painful. The rest of the answer lies in a conversation Jesus had with the Pharisee, Nicodemus.[1] In this conversation (John 3:1-21), Jesus tells Nicodemus, "Very truly, I tell you, no one can see the kingdom of God without being born from above. . . . No one can enter the kingdom of God without being born of water and Spirit. What is born of the flesh is flesh, and what is born of the Spirit is spirit" (John 3:3, 5, 6, NRSV).

To anyone who has been a Christian for any length of time, the phrase "born again" is perhaps a bit of a cliche. But not so with Nicodemus, a man who believed, as did all faithful Jews, that being born a son of Abraham assured him a place in God's kingdom. Only a Gentile who wished to join the Jewish religion needed to be "born again." Thus, Nicodemus's response (verse 4) is quite natural for him. What he needed to understand is that "the Christian's life is not a modification or improvement of the old, but a transformation of nature. There is a death to self and sin, and a new life altogether. This change can be brought about only by the effectual working of the Holy Spirit."—*The Desire of Ages*, 172.

This concept of rebirth, of a total transformation of one's nature, runs like a thread through the entire New Testament:

1. In Romans 6:1-11, Paul states that the Christian dies with Christ, then arises to a new life in which sin no longer reigns.

2. Then in 1 Corinthians 3:1, 2, he refers to recent converts as "babes in Christ." (See also Heb. 5:12-14.)

3. We learn in 2 Corinthians 5:17 that "if anyone is in Christ, there is a new creation: everything old has passed away . . . everything has become new!" (NRSV; see also Gal. 6:15.)

4. This new creation is "created to be like God in true righteousness and holiness" (Eph. 4:22-24).

5. And to Titus, Paul wrote that salvation comes not through anything we do ourselves but "according to His mercy . . . through the washing of regeneration and renewing of the Holy Spirit" (3:5, NKJV; see also 1 Pet. 1:3).

6. James says that of God's own will, "He brought us forth by the word of truth" (1:18, NKJV).

7. And finally, 1 Peter 1:22, 23, tells us that a Christian is "born again, not of corruptible seed but incorruptible, through the word of God which lives and abides forever" (NKJV).

Ezekiel 37:1-15 dramatically illustrates the new-birth experience. Like the house in Jesus' parable that stands empty, the dry bones lay lifeless. Because Israel's religion had deteriorated to a list of dos and don'ts, because they despised the bad but failed to embrace the good, some were scattered, while others were hostage to a foreign power. But Ezekiel's vision is not only a vision of death and despair. It is also a vision of life and hope, a vision of the new birth. "Thus says the Lord God to these bones: 'Surely I will cause breath to enter into you, and you shall live. I will put sinews on you and bring flesh upon you, cover you with skin and put breath in you; and you shall live. Then you shall know that I am the Lord. . . . I will open your graves and cause you to come up from your graves, and bring you into the land of Israel. . . . I will put My Spirit in you, and you shall live, and I will place you in your own land' " (Ezek. 37: 5, 6, 12, 14, NKJV).

Of this vision, Ellen White states:

> These bones represent the house of Israel, the church of God, and the hope of the church is the vivifying influence of the Holy Spirit. The Lord must breathe upon the dry bones, that they may live.
>
> The Spirit of God, with its vivifying power, must be in every human agent, that every spiritual muscle and sinew may be in exercise. Without the Holy Spirit, without the breath of God, there is torpidity [sluggishness] of conscience, loss of spiritual life. Many who are without spiritual life have their names on the church records, but they are not written in the Lamb's

book of life. They may be joined to the church, but they are not united to the Lord. They may be diligent in the performance of a certain set of duties, and may be regarded as living men; but many are among those who have "a name that thou livest, and are dead."

Unless there is genuine conversion of the soul to God; unless the vital breath of God quickens the soul to spiritual life; unless the professors of truth are actuated by heaven-born principle, they are not born of the incorruptible seed which liveth and abideth forever.—Ellen G. White Comments, *SDA Bible Commentary*, 4:1165, 1166.

Earlier in chapter 36, verses 26, 27, Ezekiel records these words, "I [God] will give you a new heart and put a new spirit in you; I will remove from you your heart of stone and give you a heart of flesh. And I will put my Spirit in you and move you to follow my decrees and be careful to keep my laws" (NIV). When this transaction occurs, God's law ceases to be a list of dos and don'ts. Because now that it is written on our hearts, we can learn to view the law from its two undergirding principles:

1. "You shall love the Lord your God with all your heart, with all your soul, and with all your mind. This is the first and great commandment' " (Matt. 22:37, 38, NKJV); and

2. "You shall love your neighbor as yourself. On these two commandments hang all the Law and the Prophets" (verses 39, 40, NKJV).

With the Holy Spirit in our hearts, our actions spring from these two "heaven-born" principles. And the fruit we bear (Gal. 5:22, 23), which composes an image of Christ's character, sprouts from the incorruptible seed planted by the Spirit Himself.

Elsewhere in the Bible

Scripture certainly is not without examples of people who experienced the guidance of the Holy Spirit in their lives. But for purposes of our discussion, perhaps the most appropriate example is that of Mary, the mother of Jesus—a woman who traveled no farther than from Palestine to Egypt (on a donkey, no less) but whose story continues to circle the globe.

When we first meet Mary in the Gospels of Matthew and Luke, she most likely is living in a house made from mud bricks or stone, topped by a flat roof consisting of timbers, reeds, or branches and smeared with mud. The inside features a hard-packed earth floor and split-level living accommodations, the upper floor, the place where the women worked and the family slept being approximately a foot higher than the lower floor. Animals stayed on the lower floor when they required shelter, and here, too, children often played.

Sabbaths most likely found Mary attending her synagogue, the center of any Jewish community that safeguarded the religion and culture of the Hebrew people. A chest that housed scrolls of the Law and the Prophets was the focal point of the main room of the synagogue. The worshipers sat facing this chest, the men on one side of the room, the women on the other or in a balcony. Mary also was probably aware of the Pharisees—the most prevalent and pious of the Jewish sects.

> The Pharisees urged upon the people an example of stern legalism characterized by strict observance of the Sabbath and of ritualistic rules of cleanliness. The round of services in the Temple at Jerusalem continued with unbending dignity and pomp, while its courtyards were filled with worshipers, beggars, money-changers, and sellers of sacrificial animals. Coming not only from the outlying reaches of Palestine, but from all over the world, thousands of pilgrims flocked to Jerusalem for the three great annual feasts of Passover and Unleavened Bread, Pentecost, and Tabernacles. . . . The Pharisees hungered for righteousness; the common people hungered for the joy of religion. . . .—*SDA Bible Commentary*, 5:55.

Certainly it was joy Mary expressed in Luke 1:46-55 after telling Elizabeth that she, Mary, had been greatly favored by God: "My soul praises the Lord and my spirit rejoices in God my Savior" (verses 46, 47). Joy is part of the fruit of the Spirit, grown as a result of the new-birth experience. And it is safe to say that Mary had experienced the new birth. Would

God have chosen a woman to fulfill such a role if she had not?

Mary's experience with the Holy Spirit involving the incarnation of Christ teaches us about the role of the Holy Spirit in transforming our own lives.

1. Matthew 1:18 is written in such a way as to let us know that Mary had nothing to do with her pregnancy other than choosing to accept the Lord's will for her life (Luke 1:38). She was the *recipient* of the Spirit's power: "She was *found to be with child through* the Holy Spirit" (Matt 1:18). Likewise, the transformation we experience when we are born again is completely the work of the Holy Spirit. Our part consists of allowing Him to do His work.

2. Paul tells us in his letter to the Galatians that Christ is formed in *us* (4:19). As we read earlier in Titus 3:5, the Holy Spirit serves as the agency of this transformation. Why should we doubt it? If the Holy Spirit could form Christ in Mary, can He not form Christ's image in us?

The last time we meet Mary, it is once again in relationship to the Holy Spirit. She, along with several other of Christ's followers, are gathered in the upper room of a private home, praying to receive the Holy Spirit as Christ promised they would (Acts 1:5, 14). However, unlike the first time we met her, we have no recorded expression of her joy as we do in Luke 1. Instead, we can only imagine how her heart sang as the disciples described their last days with her Son. As we, too, pray for the Holy Spirit to fill our empty hearthouses, to give flesh and strength to our dry, legalistic bones, we can only imagine how earnestly the mother of Jesus must have prayed that day. But we can be sure that once again her soul praised the Lord and her spirit rejoiced in her Saviour (Luke 1:46, 47).

Your story

When ten-year-old Jez Kline (his real name) learned about the parable of the haunted house in Matthew 12:43-45 and the vision in Ezekiel 36, he expressed his wish to be filled with the Spirit in the following poem.

He stands in his worst nightmare,
Feet buried in bones:
A prisoner in shackles of dead men.

In the eerie silence, he hears a voice.
He trembles.

"Speak to the bones."
He does.

He hears the rattle.
He feels the rumble.

Skulls dance to his left—hollow, faceless orbs
Fly at him to join
Bones—arms, legs, everything:
Clashing, fusing—an assembly line.

Like moss on rock,
Flesh slowly grows, creeps, covers,
The remains of once man.

Now they stand, skeleton soldiers
Frozen in form, alive yet dead.

"Speak again."
He does.

Cold winds cut through the haunted valley,
Chill his spine, swish him aside.
Breathe the Spirit into desolate beings.

Fire in the eyes
Dance in the feet
Passion in the heart
Skeleton soldiers now an army
For the Lord!

This same Spirit . . .
Once touched
A blob of nothing.

　　And then . . .

Sun, moon, and stars,
Diamonds on black velvet.

Majestic blue waves tumbling on sandy beaches.
Flowers stretching on a field, a patch-work quilt,
Kaleidoscope colors, infinite shapes.

Tall giraffes, frisky puppies, curious kittens, so much more:
A zoo without barriers, a one-of-a kind.

Man and woman, perfect in form,
Filled with the Spirit.

　　　Until . . .
　　　They　　F
　　　　　　　E
　　　　　　　L
　　　　　　　L

But they stood again
As skeleton soldiers
Awaiting the Spirit's breath.

　　　I stand, a skeleton soldier too.
　　　Breathe into me, Spirit.

Now what?

One way of filling your empty heart-house with something good after evil has been expelled from it is through Bible study.[2] Surely while they were in the upper room, Christ's followers must have studied the words He spoke to them, especially those said during their last days together on earth. That the Holy

Spirit will be active during such an activity is evidenced by the following verses:

1. "The Counselor, the Holy Spirit, whom the Father will send in my [Christ's] name, will teach you all things" (John 14:26; compare 15:26).

2. "This is what we speak, not in words taught us by human wisdom but in words taught by the Spirit, expressing spiritual truths in spiritual words. The man without the Spirit does not accept the things that come from the Spirit of God, for they are foolishness to him, and he cannot understand them, because they are spiritually discerned" (1 Cor. 2:13, 14).

3. "Take the helmet of salvation and the sword of the Spirit, which is the word of God" (Eph. 6:17).

Many approaches to Bible study have proven successful. Three of them are outlined below:

1. *The biographical approach.* Does a particular person in the Bible interest you? Use a concordance to list all the verses dealing with her/him. As you study these verses, notice the person's unique characteristics. How did these characteristics help or hinder the individual in dealing with the challenges he/she faced?

2. *The great passages approach.* Some of these could include Matthew 5–7 (the Sermon on the Mount); John 1 (the prologue to John's Gospel); Exodus 20 (the Ten Commandments) or certain of the Psalms (19, 23, 51, 90, etc). A Bible commentary will help you study the passage in its context—the whole revelation of the truth being taught and the passage's relationship to that truth. The following story illustrates the importance of doing so: England was anticipating news regarding the Battle of Waterloo. Signal lights relayed from station to station would transmit the outcome. One such station was situated at the top of Winchester Cathedral. Late one day, the message came through: "Wellington defeated." Just then a fog descended, leaving the news of Wellington's loss to sweep throughout the nation. When the fog lifted, however, the *full* report was visible: "Wellington defeated *the enemy.*"

Read the passage through several times, asking yourself: What themes does it discuss? What light does it shed on the truth being taught in the passage's context? Try to summarize each theme in a sentence or two.

3. *The thematic approach.* Use a topical concordance to list all the verses dealing with a subject of particular interest to you. Compare each verse with the other, noting the context of each. Use short phrases to summarize what each verse teaches about the subject. Use these phrases to write an overall summary of what the Bible says regarding the topic.

No matter which approach you choose, the following general tips will prove useful:

1. *Establish your priorities.* You may have to give up another activity in order to find time for Bible study.

2. *Choose a time and place.* Your mind and body should be fresh. And you should be as free from distractions as possible.

3. *Check with other sources.* In addition to the helps mentioned in the approaches above, you should purchase, over time, a Bible dictionary; maps of the Holy Land as it existed during biblical times (often these are found at the end of many Bibles); and a book or two explaining the customs, traditions, and everyday life we read about in the Bible.

4. *Pray.* The Holy Spirit will be waiting for you to seek His guidance.

5. *Reflect.* If your heart-house is waiting to be filled with something good, hang Martin Luther's "little wreath" on its door—a wreath interwoven with the following strands to help you internalize what you have studied:

- •What did I learn about God, my neighbors, and myself?
- •What reason do I now have to thank God?
- •How does what I studied help me toward salvation?
- •What does it remind me to pray for?

---

1. Jesus most likely addressed the parable in Matthew 12:43-45 specifically to the Pharisees, whose lives were free of outward sins but whose hearts still cherished evil. (See verses 22-42.)

2. Bible study differs from meditation in that Bible study is less devotional and more analytical. For example, Bible study interprets a word, while meditation will savor it. Bible study provides a foundation upon which a person can meditate. And it is always good to end a Bible study session with a quiet time of contemplation—from the head to the heart.

Chapter 5

THE HEALING TREE

The parables

It is no surprise that Jesus based many of His parables on some aspect of agriculture. During His lifetime, small family plots governed village life and economic activity. Food harvested from these plots fed the family, the village, even nearby cities. A portion of this food also helped pay taxes. Even today, over fifty percent of the population in approximately fifty-three countries are employed in agricultural fields. And even if we are not involved in such activity to earn a living, many of us have tended a backyard plot or planted a seed in a makeshift container for a science project during the early years of our formal education.

Three of Jesus' parables based on agrarian life deal in part with the work of His Holy Spirit in the new hearts we receive when we are born again (Mark 4:26-32; Luke 13:1-9). This work particularly involves the growth of Christian graces (fruit), the reproduction of Christ's character in our lives. Jesus told the parable of the unproductive fig tree (Luke 13) in response to a news report concerning an uprising in Jerusalem against Pontius Pilate, then governor of Judea. To crush the revolt, the governor commanded his soldiers to storm that part of the temple where Galilean pilgrims were offering sacrifices.

Because the Hebrew people believed that tribulation was a divine sentence passed in judgment against a person's sins, those who recounted the massacre to Jesus did so with much pride and self-righteousness. Surely those people killed were great sinners to have met with such a fate! "They expected to hear from Jesus words of condemnation for these men, who, they doubted not, richly deserved their punishment."—*Christ's Object Lessons*, p. 213. Instead, Jesus referred to their own failure to tend their heart-soil by telling a tale about a fig tree that did not bear fruit. Well aware they were of Isaiah's words, "The vineyard of the Lord Almighty is the house of Israel, and the men of Judah are the garden of his delight" (5:7). Well they knew that if they lived according to God's will, they would be "oaks of righteousness, a planting of the Lord for the display of his splendor" (61:3). Instead, "He [God] looked for a crop of good grapes, but it yielded only bad fruit" (5:2).

> The people of Christ's day made a greater show of piety than did the Jews of earlier ages, but they were even more destitute of the sweet graces of the Spirit of God. The precious fruits of character that made the life of Joseph so fragrant and beautiful, were not manifest in the Jewish nation.
>
> God in His Son had been seeking fruit, and had found none. Israel was a cumberer of the ground. Its very existence was a curse; for it filled the place in the vineyard that a fruitful tree might fill. It robbed the world of the blessings that God designed to give. The Israelites had misrepresented God among the nations. They were not merely useless, but a decided hindrance. To a great degree their religion was misleading, and wrought ruin instead of salvation.—*Christ's Object Lessons*, 215.

And as it was then, so it remains today. When people who claim to be followers of Christ fail to grow in grace, they misrepresent God to those with whom they associate. Their behavior manifests instead the fruit of another spirit as listed in Galatians 5:19-21. While such people may not grow all these evil fruits, a true Christian, through the indwelling of the Holy Spirit, will develop, over time, all of the fruit of the Spirit that is described in verses 22 and 23. What is the fruit that we can expect to develop as we let the Spirit take control of our lives? Paul lists nine characteristics of this fruit:

1. *Love*. The Greeks described four different types of love. There was *eros*, the love between a man and a woman; *philia*, the emotion we feel toward those who are nearest and dearest to our hearts; *storge*, a word used to explain the love between parents and their children; and *agape*, the word used to head the inventory of spiritual fruit.

It is no accident that such love begins Paul's list. It is that love described in the stories of the shepherd's undaunted search for one lost sheep and the father's all-embracing love for his prodigal son. It is that love pictured on a cross and echoed in the words, "Father, forgive them, for they do not know what they are doing" (Luke 23:34). And finally, it is that love that we are to reproduce as we die daily and rise to a new life in Christ. It represents the love a Christian expresses toward another person, regardless of what that person has done to the Christian. Therefore, it is a love that never seeks anything but the best for a fellow human, even if that fellow human has harmed or embarrassed you. Such love is unnatural to our human heart, and, therefore, is born only from the impact of God's *agape* love in our lives.

2. *Joy*. This type of joy is what we realize when we experience God's forgiveness. David said it well when he wrote, "You turned my wailing into dancing; you removed my sackcloth and clothed me with joy, that my heart may sing to you and not be silent. O Lord my God, I will give you thanks forever" (Ps. 30:11, 12). It is not the joy people experience as they engage in "eating and drinking" (Rom. 14:17), symbols of life's frivolous and often meaningless activities. But it is the joy we experience as we learn to trust God (Rom. 15:13). This joy becomes the lens through which we view life, thus enabling us to view even stress and trauma as avenues of growth.

3. *Peace*. This fruit matures as long as we focus on Christ, trusting only in Him (Isa. 26:3). It was this peace Paul experienced as a result of realizing that nothing could ever separate him from God's love (Rom. 8:38, 39). Such peace does not mean that the Christian life is exempt from rough roads. Instead,

this peace gives us the ability to travel such roads with confidence that God is our guide and will see us through.

Another aspect of this fruit involves our relationships with other people. It denotes not only an absence of strife, but that we act justly toward all.

4. *Longsuffering (patience, forbearance).* The Greek form of this word is used most often in the New Testament to describe the attitude of God and Jesus toward us (see Rom. 2:4; 9:22; 1 Tim. 1:18; 1 Pet. 3:20). Perhaps this attitude is best seen in the history of God's relationship with Israel. If God is so patient with us, should we not be with another? One early church leader said that this fruit of the Spirit is the grace of a person who could seek revenge, but does not.

Another Christian author wrote:

> When the sinner, in view of all his transgressions, exercises faith in God, and believes that he is pardoned because Christ has died as his sacrifice, he will be filled with gratitude to God, and will have tender sympathy toward those who, like himself, have sinned and are in need of pardon. Pride will find no place in his heart. Such faith as this will be a death-blow to a revengeful spirit. How is it possible for one who finds forgiveness, and who is daily dependent upon the grace of Christ, to turn away in coldness from those who have been overtaken in a fault and to display to the sinner an unforgiving spirit?—Ellen G. White, *Advent Review and Sabbath Herald*, 7 May 1895.

5. *Gentleness (kindness).* The same word translated in Galatians 5:22 as gentleness (or kindness) is used also in Matthew 11:29 and 30 to describe Christ's yoke. It is a yoke that does not irritate, as can the yoke that is placed over oxen. Thus, gentleness or kindness as a fruit of the Spirit suggests that our relationships with one another should imitate Christ's relationship with us. As He makes our life easier, so, too, should we share in making each other's lives easier. After all, are we not yoked together as brothers and sisters in Him?

6. *Goodness.* This is a goodness that demands a change, a response, that ripens the fruit of the Spirit. It is "uprightness in heart and life, in motives and in conduct."—*SDA Bible Commentary*, 982. Jesus displayed such goodness when He cleansed the temple. His action demanded a certain change from those who He was rebuking. As such, goodness characterizes the type of life that makes apathetic people uncomfortable in our presence. (Gentleness, on the other hand, can comfort those who are made uncomfortable by goodness.)

7. *Faith.* Our faith grows as our trust in God matures. Faith believes in the unseen and what is yet to come (Hebrews 11). It is being aware that even as we deal with the daily aspects of our lives, we are in the presence of God. And because of His presence, we will be faithful in our words and deeds toward not only Him but others, regardless of their relationship to us and God.

8. *Meekness.* This fruit of the Spirit has three meanings. It means submitting to the will of God (Matt. 5:5; 11:29; 21:5). The Christian who is meek is that person who recognizes his or her strengths and submits those strengths to the work of Christ. It also refers to being teachable, submitting your prideful opinions and theories to the truth as it is in Jesus (James 1:21). And finally, meekness means being considerate of others (1 Cor. 4:21; 2 Cor. 10:1; Eph. 4:2). When someone asked Albert Schweitzer who he thought was the greatest person on earth, he replied, "The greatest person . . . is some unknown person who at this very moment has gone to help another person in the name and with the loving Spirit of Jesus Christ."

9. *Temperance (self-control).* This fruit matures into the mastery of the self. It is the overcoming of the sinful nature described in Galatians 5:19-21. Paul discusses self-control in relationship to an athlete's discipline (1 Cor. 9:25) and the Christian's refusal to give in to impulse and desire (1 Cor. 7:9).

The purpose of self-control is that we may be fit for God, fit for ourselves, and fit to be servants of others. No wonder Paul listed it as a fruit of the Spirit. Like all the other expressions, it too flows out of love. It is not a rigid religious practice—discipline for discipline's sake. It is not dull drudgery aimed at exterminating laughter and joy. It is the doorway to true joy, true liberation from the stifling slavery of self-interest and fear. In that sense it is bound to joy, for joy is the keynote of all disciplines aimed at self-control.—Maxie D. Dunnam, *The Communicator's Commentary: Galatians, Ephesians, Philippians, Colossians, Philemon*, Lloyd J. Ogilvie, gen. ed. (Waco, Tex.: Word Books, 1982), 120.

Elsewhere in the Bible

Scripture does not detail the characteristics of the Christian church formed during and after Pentecost. But the window of Acts 1 and 2 provides us with a clear view of this new organization. Below is a list of qualities the new church possessed, based upon what we find in these two chapters. As you read this list along with chapters 1 and 2, consider how these qualities are byproducts of the fruit of the Spirit. (You might find it helpful to compare the items in the list with the description of each fruit in the previous section.)

1. The new church was a *learning* church. Upon hearing the great sermons of the apostles, the new converts willingly discarded their former religious opinions and theories.

2. It was *a praying* church. The members' newfound trust in God led them to Him on their knees. They knew they could move forward only as they moved closer to His throne.

3. It was a *sharing* church. Many of the members had come to Jerusalem to celebrate Pentecost, also called the Feast of First Fruit. When they stayed on as Christians, the generosity of those converts living in the city enabled them to do so.

4. The new church was a *joyous* church. The enthusiasm of the apostles for Christ and the difference He had made in their lives permeated their sermons as well as the minds and hearts of their listeners.

5. It was a *unified* church. Gone were selfish ambitions and jealousies, fruit of the sinful nature that caused arguments over who of the disciples was the greatest (Luke 22:24) and who among them would have the honored places in Christ's king-

dom (Mark 10:35-37). Perhaps this is the greatest evidence that the fruit of Spirit was beginning to flower and ripen among the new converts.

Your story

Approximately one out of eight Seventh-day Adventists knows someone who has AIDS, either a family member, a neighbor, or someone in the neighbor's family.[1] In congregations of approximately 200 members (any denomination), about 60 people are touched in some way by homosexuality.[2] The following story, shared by a former Seventh-day Adventist, is a poignant testimony to what the fruit of the Spirit can accomplish in even the most difficult situations.[3]

"How do you tell your parents you are HIV positive? How do you tell them the whys and the wherefores? I struggled with this dilemma for years. Then one day, the time was right. I found the words and revealed my secret. It wasn't an easy message for Mom and Dad to hear. But they immediately reassured me of their love and support.

"This revelation, however, brought many years of challenge and learning for Mom, Dad, and me. I would often feel them just watching me, trying to reconcile this new information about their son with the picture they had formed of him over the preceding thirty-five years. Most of the time, it was too great for them to deal with. They would ask me furtively how I was feeling, and I could almost hear their relief when my answer was, 'Fine.' Mom decided if I ever did become ill, she would tell friends and family I had cancer. I understood where she was coming from, but this solution was not acceptable. I explained that if my disease did progress to an AIDS diagnosis, I would tell people the truth.

"Six years passed from the time I told them, and finally, with pressure from my sister and me, my parents began to share our story with family and friends who immediately surrounded us with the support we had needed all along. Soon the mail carrier began delivering notes of love and encouragement from family members and church friends. I was pleased . . . *and* surprised. Their messages were simple. They were praying for me.

They were hoping I was doing all right. They wanted me to visit soon, and were looking forward to seeing me in church.

"About two months later, I returned home for the holidays. And what a welcome I received! Cousins, aunts, and uncles were extremely supportive. Friends stopped by. And old school chums, genuinely wanting to know how I was doing, expressed their concern.

"Of course, I was pleased and relieved. But because of the years of fearing social and church ostracism, my parents especially have been thankful for the support and acceptance they experienced. Most of society deals with social issues by either ignoring them or excluding the people involved in them. But the generous acceptance expressed to my family is one example of how the fruit of the Spirit can draw people together at the foot of the cross. The unexpected reactions of their friends and family have gone a long way to heal my parents' pain and loneliness. And the Christian expressions of love, faith, patience, and kindness continue to strengthen my own relationship with God. I believe, having learned through experience, that by withholding judgment (Matt. 7:1-5; John 5:22) and opening our hearts to lovingly accept all people, each of us can become a branch on the healing tree of God's grace."

Now what?

Submission—a total consecration of yourself to Christ—is the only way to grow the fruit of the Spirit. In fact, as seen earlier in this chapter, submission is actually part of the fruit of meekness. The more we submit to God's will, the less involved we will become with ourselves. We will become less determined to have our way, less conscious of our rights being violated. Our thoughts will turn toward others—those whom Christ came to save. *Their* good will become our goal. And we will learn to "live in harmony with one another" as did the new church. Submission is synonymous with Christ's invitation to pick up your cross and follow Him (Mark 8:34; Luke 14:27; see also chapter 2 of this book). And as is the case in all things, Jesus is our model for doing so, even unto His own cross (John 8:29; 14:9-11; 10:30; Luke 22:39-44; 23:26-46).

It is Christ's example that provides the foundation for the New Testament instruction on submission.

> Submit yourselves for the Lord's sake to every authority instituted among men. . . . To this you were called, because Christ suffered for you, leaving you an example, that you should follow in his steps. "He committed no sin, and no deceit was found in his mouth." When they hurled their insults at him, he did not retaliate; when he suffered, he made no threats. Instead, he entrusted himself to him who judges justly (1 Pet. 2:13, 21-23; see also Phil. 2:3-8).

Elsewhere, Paul prefaces his counsel on submission by saying we should "submit one to another out of reverence for Christ (Eph. 5:21). He continues with his guidance on the matter in 5:22 through 6:9 (see also Col. 3:18–4:1).

There are two things about submission we always should remember. First:

> The Epistles did not consecrate the existing hierarchical social structure. By making the command to subordination universal ["submit one to another"] they revitalized and undercut it. They called for Christians to live as citizens of a new order, and the most fundamental feature of this new order is universal subordination.—Richard J. Foster, *Celebration of Discipline: The Path to Spiritual Growth*, rev. ed. (New York, NY: HarperCollins, 1988), 120.

And secondly,

> Often the limits of submission are extremely hard to define. . . . It is not an evasion of the issue to say that in defining the limits of submission we are catapulted into a deep dependence upon the Holy Spirit. After all, if we had a book of rules to cover every circumstance in life, we would not need dependence. The Spirit is an accurate

discerner of the thoughts and intents of the heart, both yours and mine. He will be to us a present Teacher and Prophet, instructing us in what to do in every situation.—Foster, 121.

What is submission? It is Abraham and Isaac trudging up a mountain as they stare death in the face (Genesis 22). It is Mary, the mother of Jesus, responding to God's will, despite the embarrassment doing so could cause, with the words, "I am the Lord's servant. . . . May it be to me as you have said" (Luke 1:38). It is a fig tree, laden with fruit. It is the church, filled with the Holy Spirit. Is it you and I?

---

1. This is according to Dr. Harvey Elder, Chief of Infectious Diseases at Pettis Memorial Veterans Administration Hospital in Loma Linda and professor at Loma Linda University School of Medicine.

2. Virginia Ramey Mollenkott and Letha Scanzoni, *Is the Homosexual My Neighbor?* (San Francisco: HarperCollins, 1978), n.p.

3. It is not the intent of this anecdote to contradict the church's teachings regarding human sexuality. As stated, the merit of this account rests in what the fruit of the Spirit can accomplish. For further discussion on the social issues involved, we refer the reader to Ronald M. Springett, *Homosexuality in History and the Scriptures* (Silver Spring, Md.: Biblical Research Institute, General Conference of Seventh-day Adventists, 1988), and Kate McLaughlin, *My Son, Beloved Stranger* (Nampa, Idaho: Pacific Press Publishing Association, 1995).

Chapter 6

SHOES UNDER THE BED

The parable

Several nights in a row, a six-year-old girl threw a shoe under her bed. When her mother questioned this practice, the girl replied, "Teacher says if we have to kneel by our beds in the morning to look for our shoes, maybe we'll remember to say our morning prayers."

How many prayers are "under your bed," gathering dust instead of winging their way to God's ear? Or do you pray as persistently and as automatically as you seek your next breath? The parables in Luke 11:5-13 and 18:1-8 show us how important this element of Christianity is to our own personal stories of love and grace.

From the actions of the midnight friend and the determined widow, we can discern three elements of effective prayer:

1. *Effective prayer can be short, to the point, and practical.* The friend's request for bread and the widow's plea for justice were all three. The friend did not engage in a lengthy discourse, excusing himself for the late hour, his bad manners, or his friend's traveling plans. Nor did he ask for anything fanciful. He requested only the basics.

Neither was the widow's supplication any less concise, "Grant me justice against my adversary" (Luke 18:3). And to someone whose life is made miserable by inequities, what could be more basic than justice.

When we pray in a similar way, we are telling God that we

are not interested in playing games with Him, that we are not selfishly seeking our good. We wish for Him to fulfill our fundamental needs so we can provide better service for His work.

2. *Effective prayer is persistent.* The friend kept knocking until the owner of the house responded. The widow insisted on justice until she received it. Their persistence proved their desperate need and the strength of their desire to have that need met.

When we persist in prayer, we show that our faith in God's ability to provide for our needs is sincere. Such persistence can be viewed in the progression of verbs contained in Luke 11: 9. "*Ask* and it will be given to you; *seek* and you will find; *knock* and the door will be opened to you."

> **Ask, seek, knock** are not merely different metaphors for one truth, but seem rather to indicate a journey. Sometimes we are children in helplessness and can only **ask**—"with no language but a cry"; and this dependence is upon us to our journey's end. Sometimes we become pioneers and **seek**. That is right: we must not be panhandlers, merely asking, for idleness is no blessing. . . . But sometimes, whatever our pioneering hardihood, we come upon a closed door in a mountain fastness. Then we must **knock**, perhaps with bleeding knuckles at midnight.—*The Interpreter's Bible*, vol. VII (New York, N.Y.: Abingdon-Cokesbury Press, 1951), 328.

3. *Effective prayer is expectant.* The friend expected to receive bread. The widow expected to receive justice. Their persistence proved their expectancy. If we do not expect God to answer our prayers, why pray? A lack of such hopefulness displays a lack of sincerity, a lack of faith. Perhaps James said it best when he wrote, "Ask in faith, never doubting, for the one who doubts is like a wave of the sea, driven and tossed by the wind; for the doubter, being double-minded and unstable in every way, must not expect to receive anything from the Lord" (James 1:6-8, NRSV).

Elsewhere in the Bible

Both the Old and New Testaments highlight the importance of meaningful, persistent, and expectant prayer. In the Old Testament alone, we can read 190 prayers. This number does not include such psalms whose titles suggest they were composed as prayers (Ps. 17, 86, 90, 102, etc.)

In the New Testament, we learn that prayer was the secret to the church's growth. The book of Acts mentions prayer nineteen times (Acts 1:14; 2:42; 3:1; 6:4; 10:4, 31; 12:5; 16:13, 16; etc), while a glance reveals that the opening verses of Paul's letters consisted of prayers.

But numbers alone do not attest to the importance of prayer. Jesus' example teaches us that prayer is significant because it is a form of intimate communication between the Father and His children. In Mark 14:36, Jesus addresses God as "Abba," a Hebrew word for father used to express close relationship. (It is interesting to note that He used this term of endearment when being His Father's Son was causing Him great suffering.)

Daniel's example of prayer in Daniel 9:3-19 informs us that a sincere prayer can exert more power than any head of state:

> Daniel on his knees was a mightier man than Darius on his throne. Daniel was in the service of the King of kings; was admitted to the audience-chamber of the Most High; and received the announcements of the Divine will. Darius *now* mainly serves as a landmark on the course of time to indicate a date; Daniel is still the teacher and moulder of men.—*The Pulpit Commentary*, vol. 13, H. D. M. Spence and Joseph S. Exell, eds. (Peabody, Mass.: Hendrickson Publishers, n.d.), 284.

These verses also describe at least four more elements of effective prayer.

1. *Prayer should be based on a knowledge of God's will.* Daniel's desire to understand the vision in chapter 8 is based on his knowledge of Jeremiah's prophecy concerning God's plan

to end Israel's captivity (9:2, 3). Such knowledge made Daniel's prayer all the more necessary. The time for Israel's freedom depended in part on their spiritual readiness. Thus, Daniel's prayer becomes an integral part of God's plan. Daniel most likely did not know the full importance of his plea. But hope in the fulfillment of Jeremiah's prophecy motivated his cry for help. He knew that if God promised to bless Israel, he could be expectant in his prayer.

2. *Prayer should gain its inspiration from God's character.* Israel's sins may frustrate Daniel. But it is God's mercy that motivates his plea (verses 4, 5). After all, is he not praying to the God who keeps His covenant of love with those who love and obey Him? Daniel can pray for God to look with favor on Israel and the sanctuary not because of Israel's righteousness, but because of God's grace (verse 18).

3. *Prayer should empty us of ourselves and identify us with others.* Daniel confessed with humility and honesty all manner of wrongdoing, regarding the sins of kings, priests, and judges as his own. Robed in sackcloth and adorned with ashes, he seeks to empty himself of pride and self-righteousness. Interceding for his fellow Hebrews, he seeks to carry their burden.

4. *Prayer must include earnest pleading.* "Turn away your anger and your wrath" (verse 16).

"Hear the prayers and petitions of your servant. . . . Look with favor on your desolate sanctuary" (verse 17).

"Give ear, O God, and hear; open your eyes"(verse 18).

"O Lord, listen! O Lord, forgive! O Lord, hear and act!. . . O my God, do not delay" (verse 19).

These heartfelt cries for God's guidance permeate Daniel's prayer and provide a pounding drumbeat toward its conclusion. Such a persistent rhythm helps us to envision Daniel on his knees, pleading with God, helping to change the course of lives through prayer.

Your story
The following personal account of a dedicated teacher further shows how persistent, sincere prayer can change lives. What elements of successful prayer are evident in this

person's experience?

"Only a few days into the new school year and already I dreaded getting up in the morning and facing Vicki. She had entered my classroom an angry preteen, her attitude damaging the disposition of everyone in my multigrade room. *What do I do with Vicki*, I often wondered?

"As a teacher, I know I have a wonderful opportunity to witness about Jesus to impressionable students for 180 days a year. So I wondered what He would do about Vicki if He were the teacher. He would smile at her and melt her heart probably. I, on the other had, seemed to agitate her more every day.

"One morning as I walked through the door, I once again offered a silent prayer for Vicki. She had every reason to distrust the world and the adults who dealt with her. Nonetheless, that didn't give her the right to ruin everyone's day. Another prayer heavenward and the day began.

"September passed into October, and I found myself wishing for May. I had used all my teacher tactics acquired over twelve years. But still I could not reach Vicki. She continued her screaming tirades and hate-filled whispers. Could it be too late for her?

" 'My mother says I can go to school wherever I want, and I sure don't want it to be this place.' Vicki slammed her books on her desk and flounced heavily onto her chair. Another day. Another prayer for Vicki.

"The leaves needed raking in front yards, snow shovels came out of storage, and students began memorizing lines for the Christmas program. The only thing not changing seemed to be Vicki. Students began to complain that they were tired of being patient with her.

"One evening a week I attended a graduate class at the local university. There were eighteen of us, mostly teachers, from public and private schools all over the city. A woman I knew only as Betty was one of my classmates. One night, my mind strayed from the lecture to ponder Vicki once again. Instantly after I offered another prayer for help, I heard the words whispered in my ear, 'Talk to Betty.' I tried turning my attention back to the professor. But again I received the impression, 'Talk to Betty about Vicki.' There was no real opportunity to visit with my classmate that evening, so I left, wondering if my obsession with solving my Vicki problem was making me delusional!

"When Vicki arrived the next morning, I greeted her with a smile and suddenly asked, 'Do you remember your teacher's name from last year?'

"Vicki brightened, 'I sure do! She's the best teacher I ever had! I'll always love Ms. Thomas!'

" 'Do you know her first name?' I questioned.

" 'Sure. It's Betty.' Vicki beamed.

"I tried to remain calm, 'Vicki, what does Ms. Thomas look like?'

"Vicki went on to describe the Betty in my class. Could it be? Was it possible I was taking a class with Vicki's beloved teacher? What are the odds of the two of us getting together in an obscure graduate class in the second largest city in the state? Impossible!

"The next week Betty and I were supposed to be discussing a topic assigned by our teacher. But I had to know! 'Do you know Vicki Woods?' I blurted out.

"Betty almost leapt from her chair. 'Do you know Vicki? I love Vicki. She was one of my favorite students. Where is she? How is she doing?' Betty's exuberant questions flowed while I tried to catch my breath. Finally she stopped, and I found my voice. I described all the trouble I was having with her former top student. Now it was Betty's turn to go into shock. She informed me I wasn't getting to see any of *her* Vicki. Even though we talked for some time, I still hadn't discovered how to help Vicki. But I kept praying.

"The next morning, I couldn't wait to tell Vicki I knew her former teacher and that she had told me so many good things about her. Vicki had her own handful of questions about Ms. Thomas. We actually had a nice conversation! And soon life began to change. Vicki began to be more friendly to the rest of us. In just a week's time she'd gone from a roaring lioness to merely a squalling cat.

"After my next two classes, Vicki quizzed me about Ms.

Thomas. Then the course ended, and I worried that the old Vicki would return. I shouldn't have, however, for God had answered my prayers in a way I never could have foreseen.

"Vicki is now usually a purring kitten. I have finally seen the wonderful young lady Betty described to me. May has arrived, and I will regret losing my much prayed-about Vicki. How thankful I am for the power of persistent, earnest prayer."

Now what?

In this chapter, the stories about a persistent friend, widow, prophet, and teacher hopefully have inspired you to examine your own prayer life. But is it really a life separate from everything else you do? The idea of persistency seems to imply that it is not. Prayer—communication with God—is the chief ingredient of a healthful relationship with Him. Do you have friends with whom you never or seldom communicate, except when you desire favors from them? Then you have no friends in the true sense of the word! When praying becomes a natural response to the work of God's love and grace in your life, it will occur as naturally and as often as breathing. Then you will live, as it were, in an attitude of prayer.

To live such a life automatically takes practice. Perhaps it even means you will have to throw your shoes under the bed. But one thing is sure. The more you pray, the more you will pray. This is so, because the more you pray, the more you will "begin to think God's thoughts after him; to desire the things he desires, to love the things he loves, to will the things he wills."—Richard J. Foster, *Celebration of Discipline: The Path to Spiritual Growth*, rev. ed. (New York, N.Y.: HarperCollins, 1988), 33.

In her book *Steps to Christ*, Ellen White highlights the significance of prayer by stating that "prayer is the opening of the heart to God as to a friend" and that "the darkness of the evil one encloses those who neglect to pray" (93,94). How important it is, then, to maintain the lines of communication between you and God. To help you do so, here are a few suggestions describing different ways to pray. Perhaps they will spark some ideas of your own.

1. *The breathing prayer*. This method of prayer is an excellent way to relax when you are angry or frustrated. As you breathe in, pray, "God, please enter my heart." As you breathe out, pray, "Take away my anger (fear, frustration, hurt, etc.)." As you inhale next, say, "I breathe in Your peace (power, grace, etc.)." Continue in this manner until you are calmed and completely focused on the Saviour instead of the event that caused the need to pray. Thus even the very act of breathing becomes an act of prayer.

2. *The silent prayer*. Begin by saying, "Lord, I'm here. Speak to me." Then do not say anything more. Instead, concentrate on a specific aspect of God—His love, mercy, patience, etc. What thoughts come to your mind regarding this characteristic? What biblical stories come to mind that illustrate this aspect of God's character? What do you hear God "saying" about Himself and His desire to be active in your life?

3. *The physical prayer*. Are you dreading a specific chore? The laundry? Changing the oil in the car? Pray while you are doing it. Pray while you run, walk. Pray while you look for your shoes under the bed. Talking with God this way sanctifies every part of life, creating out of every activity an opportunity to meet with Him.

4. *The sunrise prayer*. "His compassions never fail. They are new every morning" (Lam. 3:22, 23). When you are awake enough to make sense, pray for the day ahead of you, for strength to overcome the trials and temptations which may arise, for opportunities to help others. Pray that you will discern God's will for the hours yet untarnished by our stubbornness and pride.

> The first moments of the new day are not the time for our own plans and worries, not even for our zeal to accomplish our own work, but for God's liberating grace, God's sanctifying presence. . . . Before the heart unlocks itself for the world, God wants to open it for himself; before the ear takes in the countless voices of the day, it should hear in the early hours the voice of the Creator and Redeemer. . . .

Before our daily bread should be the daily Word. Only thus will the bread be received with thanksgiving. Before our daily work should be the morning prayer. Only thus will the work be done as the fulfillment of God's command. The morning must yield an hour of quiet time for prayer and common devotion. That is certainly not wasted time. How else could we prepare ourselves to face the tasks, cares, and temptations of the day? And although we are often not "in the mood" for it, such devotion is an obligatory service to the One who desires our praises and prayers, and who will not otherwise bless our day but through his Word and our prayers.—Dietrich Bonhoeffer, *Meditating on the Word*, edited and translated by David McI. Gracie (Cambridge, Mass.: Cowley Publications, 1986), 38, 39.

5. *The sunset prayer.* Sometime in the evening, before you are desperately seeking your pillow, take a few minutes to thank God for helping you through the day. Mention specific instances when you felt His presence. And tell Him what pleasure or comfort a particular person, item, or event gave you. Recalling such mercies with the One who provided them might prove more beneficial than a sleeping pill. It surely will help you to remember that, despite everything bad the day might have brought, God's caring, thoughtful hand is ever writing your story of love and grace, bringing it to a fruitful conclusion.

Chapter 7

FEEDING ON GOODNESS

The parable

In temperate climates around the world, gardeners seek to ease their frustration with the lion's tooth, commonly known as the dandelion. The deep notches, or teeth, of the plant's leaves are not the source of frustration, nor are the plant's sunny yellow, disc-shaped flowers. Instead, the gnashing of human teeth is caused by the taproot of this weed. This root is thick, pointed, and long (sometimes up to three feet), with hairlike roots branching from it. Such a system enables the dandelion to cling so tenaciously to the soil that to rid the landscape of it, gardeners must dig deeply to destroy all of the tap. Any little bit of this root left will produce an even more vigorous plant.

Pride is to the soil of our heart what the dandelion is to a beloved patch of land.

1. Like the dandelion's root, pride's taproot grows deep, its hairlike roots permeating every aspect of our life. All of pride must be extracted from our hearts, or what is left behind will yield a stronger stock of that emotion.

2. Just as the seed of the dandelion will grow anywhere, even in sidewalk cracks, so will pride. Some of the most unlikely people have allowed the seed of arrogance to root in their hearts.

3. Dandelions prevent a gardener from enjoying the more fruitful aspects of gardening. Likewise, pride in our own abilities prevents us from growing the fruit of the Spirit.

.

4. The dandelion grows well even in horrid conditions. But it flourishes in good soil. So does pride feed on goodness. The Pharisee's prayer in Jesus' parable (Luke 18:9-14) provides an excellent example of this.

That the Pharisee was so proud of his goodness he even bragged about himself to God is not such a curious thing when we understand the nature of his religion. The word *Pharisee* literally means "the separated one." No ordinary person could ever keep the thousands of regulations the scribes and rabbis drew up to supposedly clarify God's law. Thus the Pharisees separated themselves from life's daily activities in order to do so. Eventually, however, they began to believe they were better than everyone else, and that ordinary people who could not keep the law as carefully were sinful.

But such a religion is synonymous with the empty-house religion we studied about in Matthew 12:43-45, and it shows up negative on the balance sheet. Instead of focusing on God, the Pharisee's theology focused on what he himself did *not* do. He did *not* commit adultery, he did *not* steal, he did *not* do evil, he did *not* collect taxes. He did *not* . . . He did *not* . . . . He did *not* . . . .

All of this is the opposite of true goodness, which Matthew 7:12 describes, "Do to others what you would have them do to you."

> The standard of the golden rule is the true standard of Christianity; anything short of it is a deception. A religion that leads men to place a low estimate upon human beings, whom Christ has esteemed of such value as to give Himself for them; a religion that would lead us to be careless of human needs, sufferings, or rights, is a spurious religion.—*Thoughts From the Mount of Blessings*, 136, 137.

But even the golden rule received negative expression in the Hebrew religion. Hillel, one of the most respected rabbis who lived a generation before Jesus, is said to have written, "What is hateful to you, do not do to your neighbor." When expressed this way, it becomes a fairly easy command to observe. You simply do not do particular things. But the end product is a Pharisee—a person charmed and delighted by his or her own abilities.

However, when stated the way Jesus proclaimed it, the golden rule infers we must make a conscious effort to be as compassionate and patient toward others as we would have them be toward us. This makes our behavior toward others a matter of doing as opposed to *not* doing. When the balance sheet is examined, Christ will not ask, "What did you *not* do?" but "What did you *do?*" (Matt. 25:31-46).

> In your association with others, put yourself in their place. Enter into their feelings, their difficulties, their disappointments, their joys, and their sorrows. Identify yourself with them, and then do to them as, were you to exchange places with them, you would wish them to deal with you. . . . It is another expression of the law, "Thou shalt love thy neighbor as thyself." Matthew 22:39. . . .

> The golden rule is the principle of true courtesy, and its truest illustration is seen in the life and character of Jesus. Oh, what rays of softness and beauty shone forth in the daily life of our Saviour! What sweetness flowed from His very presence! The same spirit will be revealed in His children. Those with whom Christ dwells will be surrounded with a divine atmosphere. Their white robes of purity will be fragrant with perfume from the garden of the Lord. Their faces will reflect light from His, brightening the path for stumbling and weary feet.—*Thoughts From the Mount of Blessings*, 134, 135.

In this case, the end product is a person, who because of focusing on Christ, recognizes his or her great deficiencies, and the need for his or her relationships to be filled with Christ's compassion and patience.

Elsewhere in the Bible

The Pharisee's prayer tells us that pride involves judging others, holding their behavior under the microscope of your own goodness and abilities to prove you are better than they. Such was the case with Miriam and Aaron when they used Moses' wife as an excuse to protest that their opinion had not been sought regarding the selection of the seventy elders (Numbers 11 and 12). Even before there was such a label as *pharisaical*, their words displayed such pleasure with themselves, "Has the Lord spoken only through Moses? . . . Hasn't he also spoken through us?" (12:2). Ellen White wrote that this same prideful note echoes the "same evil that first brought discord in heaven" (*Patriarchs and Prophets*, 382).

> Little by little Lucifer came to indulge the desire for self-exaltation. [Ezek. 28:17 and Isaiah 14:13, 14 quoted.] Though all his glory was from God, this mighty angel came to regard it as pertaining to himself. Not content with his position, though honored above the heavenly host, he ventured to covet homage due alone to the Creator. . . . And coveting the glory with which the infinite Father had invested His Son, this prince of angels aspired to power that was the prerogative of Christ alone.—*Patriarchs and Prophets*, 35.

How unlikely that the covering cherub, who resided "on the holy mount of God" and was blameless in his ways (Ezek. 28:12-15), should succumb to pride. How unlikely that the young woman who outwitted one of Pharaoh's cruel laws (Exod. 1:1–2:10) and that the man, who with Moses, brought yet another Pharaoh to his knees (Exod. 7:1, 2) should surrender not to the Power who guarded them against evil, but to that evil itself. Such, however, is the nature of the dandelion. It grows in the most unlikely places.

The dangerous nature of pride is attested to by the nature of punishment visited upon Miriam—leprosy.

Aaron was . . . severely rebuked in Miriam's punishment. Now, their pride humbled in the dust, Aaron confessed their sin, and entreated that his sister might not be left to perish by that loathsome and deadly scourge. In answer to the prayers of Moses the leprosy was cleansed. Miriam was, however, shut out of the camp for seven days. . . . In respect for her high position, and in grief at the blow that had fallen upon her, the whole company abode in Hazeroth, awaiting her return.—*Patriarchs and Prophets*, p. 385.

The next and also the last time we hear of Miriam is the brief mention of her death in Numbers 20:1. Did pride and its effects lay such a buoyant person so low that her accomplishments for God amounted to nothing after the incident in Numbers 11 and 12? Of course, we can only speculate, and probably we should not do that for long. But it is worth pausing to think about the damage pride can do. The tax collector left the temple court justified. The supposed man of God did not.

Your story
Carol shares with us how pride got in her way of working for the Lord. When you finish reading about her experience, you will know why she no longer refers to herself as a soulwinner, but a seedsower!

"Looking out over the faces of the people gathered on Sabbath afternoon to hear me talk about witnessing filled me with great satisfaction and personal pride. I was feeling that I had the knack for soul winning and for teaching others how to do it.

"I had become a Christian at forty-eight years of age and had won my two grown children to the Lord. As the years passed, they each married a non-Christian. But through much prayer, manipulation, and pressure on my part, these spouses also became baptized.

"Then I fell head-over-heels in love with an atheist. After dating for five and one-half years, I was convinced he had become a Christian. So when he asked me to marry him, I said Yes, even though I knew it would take a while to find the right

Seventh-day Adventist Church for him to be baptized in.

"By this time, I was fairly swollen with pride. *Now my children and I will all be married to Christian Seventh-day Adventists, and we will all live happily, forever and forever*, I thought. *Now I can teach other people how to win their loved ones to the Lord too.* This would give me a lot of status in the church!

"But I had been married only six months when my happily-ever-after life began to unravel. Because my husband grew increasingly angry over the way some 'Christian' Seventh-day Adventists treated him, he refused to be baptized. At one point, he even threatened to leave me if I would not change my membership to a completely different denomination. As much as I loved my husband, I desired to remain true to my faith. Fortunately, he soon relented, and we did not separate.

"Next, my daughter and son-in-law moved back to Ohio, where they lived with his non-Christian family because he was unable to find a job. Through pressure from them and peers, he became bitter toward the church and stopped attending. He finally said he would leave my daughter if she did not leave the church too. She refused, so my son-in-law found someone else and remarried.

"Finally, my son's wife had a 'real' conversion experience during one of his evangelistic campaigns. As it turned out, she had only agreed to baptism so she could marry him. I had suspected this, but my pride could not allow me to admit that my son, the preacher, was married to a non-Christian.

"Needless to say, my balloon was thoroughly deflated. I felt like the last person in the world who could win souls to Jesus. Then one day I came across this verse. 'Go home to your family and tell them how much the Lord has done for you, and how he has had mercy on you.' So the man went away and began to tell in the Decapolis how much Jesus had done for him. And all the people were amazed (Mark 5:19, 20). Incredible! Jesus doesn't expect us to *win* people to the Lord as much as He expects us to *plant seeds* by telling others what He has done for us!

"My husband once compared my soul-winning tactics to a bulldozer. 'You bombarded people with the truth, then sat back, self-assured that you were right, and waited for them to accept Jesus on *your* terms!'

"But now I have learned to pray more, asking the Holy Spirit to guide me (Luke 11:13). I also spend much more time praying for people who are not Christians, asking God to help me love them so much they will see Jesus through my actions. Each day I ask the Lord to lead me to someone I can share Him with. It's amazing how sometimes this works so conveniently into the conversation when I least expect it. Also, I have learned *always* to give God the glory for any progress that might be made toward bringing someone to salvation. Never should I receive any credit! It is the Holy Spirit and Jesus' sacrifice that will win people to Him, not the efforts of one 'little old lady.'

"Now, instead of giving seminars, I prefer to sit in someone's kitchen, sharing with them stories of God's grace and love. One day, as I sat across the table from a long-time friend discussing the wonders of God's love, she shared with me how guilty I used to make her feel when she attended my seminars. 'No matter how hard I tried, I could never win souls like you!' Now, however, we both understand that while pride can make you think you are a soul winner, it is humility that actually sows the seed!"

Now what?

Humility. It is recognizing that you are a sinner whose only hope is Christ. It is allowing the Holy Spirit to cultivate your heart-soil so His fruit will grow strong and healthy. The parable contrasting the prayers of the Pharisee and the tax collector shows how necessary it is. But how do you uproot the lion of pride to achieve it?

Unfortunately, there is no one equation that when followed exactly equals humility. There are certain things, however, that lend themselves to the development of this Christian grace.

1. Carol's experience in the Your story section shows us that

God's work of refining and purifying must go on until His servants are so humbled, so dead to self, that, when called into active service, their eye will be single to His glory. . . . God brings men over the ground again and again, increasing the pressure until perfect humility and a transformation of character bring them into harmony with Christ and the spirit of heaven, and they are victors over themselves.—*Testimonies for the Church*, 4:86; emphasis supplied.

Notice the connection in this quotation between humility and the transformation of character.

2. As the Pharisee's behavior exhibits, pride separates us from our Saviour. But the "work of refining and purifying" hopefully compels us to seek Him. As we *draw closer to Him*, we will become increasingly aware of His unblemished nature and our sinfulness. As this awareness increases, the likelihood of exalting ourselves, of feeling we are better than others, will decrease.

In order to preserve humility, it would be well to remember how we appear in the sight of a holy God, who reads every secret of the soul, and how we should appear in the sight of our fellow men if they all knew us as well as God knows us. For this reason, to humble us, we are directed to *confess our faults*, and improve this opportunity to subdue our pride.—*Testimonies for the Church*, 3:211; emphasis supplied.

The life of Paul demonstrates this principle. In the beginning of his work for God, he refers to himself as "Paul, an apostle" (Gal. 1:1). During the height of his work, he writes in 1 Corinthians 15:9, 10, "I am the least of the apostles and do not even deserve to be called an apostle, because I persecuted the church of God. But by the grace of God I am what I am, and his grace to me was not without effect." Then in Ephesians 3:8, toward the end of his career, he states, "I am less than the least of all God's people." Finally, he writes to Timothy, "Christ Jesus came into the world to save sinners—of whom I am the worst" (1 Tim. 1:15).

3. As we discussed in chapters 3 and 4, *meditation*—especially on the life of Christ—and *Bible study* are excellent ways

of drawing close to Him. "*What we learn of the Great Teacher of truth* will be enduring; it will not savor of self-sufficiency, but *will lead to humility and meekness* and the work that we do will be wholesome, pure, and ennobling, because wrought in God."—*Testimonies for the Church*, 5:647, 648; emphasis supplied.

From such studying, we will discern the greatest definition of humility—the Son of God being born in a stable, working as a carpenter, washing His disciples' feet, dying a criminal's death.

Chapter 8

TALENTED HARMONY

The parable

One day, the famous conductor, Sir Michael Costa, was holding a rehearsal. The choir was singing heartily, accompanied by hundreds of instruments. But the piccolo player, deciding to take a "breather," stopped playing. Surely the notes from the smallest of woodwinds would not be missed. Suddenly, however, Costa demanded, "Where's the piccolo?" The sound of that one small instrument *was* necessary to the harmony of the music.

The parable of the three servants (Matt. 25:14-30) teaches us that everyone's talents, no matter how small, are necessary to insure that the Lord's work operates harmoniously. To study this parable more thoroughly, we will take a look at the following four aspects of the opportunities God gives us to use our talents. These aspects are: (1) the responsibility with which God entrusts us; (2) how we respond to that responsibility; (3) the judgment we will face regarding how we reacted to our responsibility; and (4) the reward we receive for how we use our talents.

1. *Our responsibility.* The master who is going away for a long time represents Christ and the time between His return to heaven and His second advent. The master's servants symbolize us—members of His church with whom He has entrusted varied skills to be used in fulfilling the gospel commission (Matt. 28:19, 20).

The levels of responsibility the master gives each of his servants varies. But the master's expectations of each servant does not. As their master, he has the right to assume that each of them will do the best he can with his talents and the opportunities that come his way to invest them. It is not *the amount* each one has, but what each one *does* with the amount he has.

These levels of responsibility represent the vast extent of abilities among church members. Members also differ in opportunity and privilege. Some were raised in Christian homes, where family worships began and ended their days. Sabbath School and church attendance happily ended one week and started another. Perhaps as adults, they even work for the church. Others, however, may be the only Christians in their families, workplace, or town. But once again, it is not the amount one has been given, but the effort one extends in utilizing it.

The servants with the five and two talents did not earn equal profits. But their gain was equal in percentage. Likewise, Christians with various skills and opportunities will produce various results with equal faithfulness and dedication.

2. *Our reaction.* The servant with the five talents "went and traded with them, and made another five talents" (verse 16, NKJV). The context suggests that he conducted business over time. He did not just make a single wise investment, then relax, thinking he had done what was expected of him. Perhaps he even kept trading for as along as his master was gone.

The same is true of the servant who received two talents. Even though he had less to trade with, he did so as diligently as the servant who had more. Their starting points were not equal, but their dedication to fulfilling their master's command was.

Then there is the servant with the least who hid what little he had in the ground. But receiving the smallest amount did not exempt him from increasing it. The master still required him to increase it—the same requirement he placed upon the other two servants.

Most of us, unfortunately, are like this third servant. We think our abilities are minimal, and like the piccolo player, will not be missed if we bury them unused under the daily routine of our personal lives. But how many major woodwinds can there be in one orchestra? How many soloists in one choir? The answers to these questions imply that the majority of us are one-talent servants. But our Master does not leave it there. He presents us *all* with opportunities to use our abilities. The indwelling of His Holy Spirit equally enables *each* of us to render loyal service.

> There is no lack of great works going on for our Lord to which we may safely attach ourselves, and in which our talent is rather invested for us than left to our own discretion. The parable does not acknowledge any servants who have absolutely nothing. There is something to be done which precisely you can do, something by doing which you will please him whose pleasure in you will fill your nature with gladness; it is given to you to increase the Lord's goods. . . . Money is made for circulation; so is grace. Yet some men might as well have no grace for all the good it does; it is carefully wrapped up, as if encounter with the world would fret its edges and lower its value. . . . You cannot possibly have just so much grace and no more; it must grow, or it will die.—*The Pulpit Commentary*, H. D. M. Spence and Joseph S. Exell, eds. (Peabody, Mass.: Hendrickson Publishers, n.d.), 15:500, 501.

3. *Our judgment.* At long last the master returns. And when he does, he reviews the accounts of his servants. Even though the first two received unequal amounts to work with, the master's assessment of their endeavors was the same, " 'Well done, good and faithful servant! You have been faithful with a few things' " (verses 21, 23). Such a pronouncement praises not so much the profit, but the servants' perspective regarding their master and what the master gave them. The servants' "good and faithful" character expressed itself in a job "well done."

The one-talent servant did not need the master to pronounce him guilty. He condemned himself with his own feeble excuses.

But lest there be any doubt, the master judged the servant's character with the words *wicked, lazy,* and *worthless* (verses 26, 30). What a shock to those of us one-talented church members who claim we are unneeded! Jesus here tells us our humility is feigned! Do not wait until He returns to hear His assessment of your account. Realize now, before it is too late—Jesus cares more about *how* you use what He has given you than *what* He has given you. *You* are the only one worried about the latter!

4. *Our reward.* Just as the judgment was the same for the first two servants, so was their reward. Because of their faithfulness in a few things, their master would put them in charge of many things (verses 21, 23). Their fortune increased again! But the third servant, already minus a profit, also lost what the master originally had given him (verse 28). Thus a universal rule of life is once again confirmed: Use it or lose it. If we do not exercise, we gradually lose the use of our muscles. If a person sings well but does not practice, she or he will lose the ability to do so. The only way to keep the skills God has given us is to use them on His behalf in serving others.

The other part of the reward concerns the fruit of the Spirit (Gal. 5:22, 23). Both the first and the second servant were invited to share the *joy* of their lord (Matt. 25: 21, 23). As Christians working for our Master, we will experience delight not only as our talents increase through use, but simply because we are working for Him. A life dedicated to God's service is a life full of accomplishment, satisfaction, and above all, joy.

We also will enter into the joy of our Lord when in heaven we will see those who have been saved, in part, because of how we employed our talents. "Our reward for working with Christ in this world is the greater power and wider privilege of working with Him in the world to come."—*Christ's Object Lessons,* 361.

What of the one-talent servant? His destiny is recorded in verse 30.

Surely this story inspires us to live a courageous faith, to be bold in the use of our talents. We are assured of the outcome if we do not. But we also are assured of the outcome if we do.

Elsewhere in the Bible

Scripture is full of advice about taking advantage of opportunities while they are available. Solomon wrote "Cast your bread upon the waters, for after many days you will find it again," and "Sow your seed in the morning, and at evening let not your hands be idle, for you do not know which will succeed, whether this or that, or whether both will do equally well" (Eccl. 11:1, 6). Jesus consistently called upon people to take advantage of spiritual opportunities. One of His calls is found in John 12:35, 36.

Quite possibly one of the most fascinating and charming people in the Bible who took advantage of an opportunity to use what he had for Christ is a nameless young boy. In the process, he helped to feed a crowd of at least 5,000. The multitude following Jesus was hungry, and His concern for them was evident (John 6:5). Philip concluded from a quick scan of the scene that it would take more than eight months' wages to buy enough bread to feed everyone (verse 7). But Andrew found "a boy with five small barley loaves and two small fish" (verse 9). What good, however, was so little food when there were so many people?

It is this bread that gives us the only real clue about the boy. Because barley was a great deal less expensive than wheat, it was the staple of the poor. This fact makes the boy's generosity even more remarkable. There might not be anything to eat when he returned home. Yet he was willing to share his meager supply with Jesus so others might be fed as well. What had convinced the boy to even consider such a thing? Perhaps he had witnessed the miraculous signs Jesus performed on the sick (verse 2). We cannot be sure. But we can be sure that this boy, with his supposedly inconsequential amount of food, proved what the one-talent servant in the parable did not—the important thing isn't what you have, but how you use it.

The next time you start thinking there isn't much you can do with the little you have, why not be encouraged by this young hero instead. You might just go down in the record books. But even if you don't, you will undoubtedly have helped someone who may in turn help someone who may in turn. . . . And the ripples widen.

Your story

"I'm an organizer," states Marilyn matter-of-factly. "I have a knack for putting great messes in order. But until I met Steve, I had no idea I could use that talent to work for God."

Marilyn continues her story, complete with a surprise ending. "Steve's wife had been sick for such a long time, that when she died, there was a flood of medical and funeral bills flowing in daily. Poor Steve. The tears made it difficult and, at times, impossible to decipher them all. A neighbor who was trying to help Steve goes to the same church I do. One Sabbath, he was telling me about the situation. 'Maybe I could help,' I volunteered. So the next day, I found myself sitting at Steve's kitchen table facing an intimidating mound of paperwork.

"For the next few weeks, Steve and his neighbor left me to wade through the clutter. After several calls to doctors, insurance companies, and hospitals, it became clear which accounts had been settled and which had not. Often during this time, the three of us would eat out after a hard session of work. Or sometimes Steve would have a big pot of homemade soup ready for us to enjoy. To our surprise, Steve started attending church with us. After the services, we would have a picnic in a nearby park. During these outings, the three of us enjoyed discussing our experiences and beliefs. Steve talked about why he didn't believe in God.

"When I tucked the last bill into its proper file, and at last we could see the table, Steve commented, 'Marilyn, you've saved my life helping me with all this paperwork. I never could have managed it alone.' He also told me how he appreciated my straightforward talk about Christ and that I stood firm whenever he talked disparagingly about God. 'You accepted me and respected my right to believe as I do, even though my atheistic talk must have offended you at times.'

"Helping Steve get his paperwork organized during his time of grief was an opportunity that fell across my path. And I used my talents the best I could. I even was able to share some thoughts with him about what Christ does for me. Steve and I remained close friends through the years. Now he is a Christian, and we are both happily married—to each other!"

Now what?

The story of the talented servants is about stewardship. And stewardship is about our "responsibility for, and use of, everything entrusted to" us "by God—life, physical being, time, talents and abilities, material possessions, opportunities to be of service to others, and his knowledge of truth."—*SDA Encyclopedia*, rev. ed., 10:1425.

The book *Seventh-day Adventists Believe* . . . eloquently describes the spiritual growth process that occurs through stewardship.

More than anything else living a Christian life means surrender—a giving up of ourselves and an accepting of Christ. As we see how Jesus surrendered and gave Himself up for us, we cry out, "What can I do for You?"

Then, just when we think we have made a full commitment, a full surrender, something happens that demonstrates how shallow our commitment is. As we discover new areas of our lives to turn over to God, our commitment grows. Then, ever so gently, He brings to our attention another area where self needs to surrender. And so life goes on through a series of Christian recommitments that go deeper and deeper into our very selves, our lifestyles, how we act and react.

When we give all that we are and have to God, to whom it all belongs anyway (1 Cor. 3:21-4:2), He accepts it but then puts us back in charge of it, making us stewards, or caretakers, of everything that we "possess." Then our tendency to live comfortable, selfish lives is broken by our realization that our Lord was naked, imprisoned, and a stranger. And His enduring "Go ye therefore, and teach all nations" makes the church's activities—sharing, teaching, preaching, baptizing—more precious to us. Because of Him we seek to be faithful stewards.—269.

What does it mean in practical terms to "give all that we are and have to God"? The list below discusses several different "talents" we all can use and is based on the fact that whatever we do for others, we do for Christ (Matt. 25:21-40). Included are little things (like the loaves and fish) that can make a big difference in someone's day, little touches of lovingkindness that Christ would do if He were here, but that we must now do in His place. Let these suggestions be spring-boards for ideas of your own.

1. *Give an ear.* A co-worker comes by while you are frantically attempting to meet a deadline. He is obviously distressed and wants to talk. Do you brush him off? Or do you listen to his problem? Do you express an interest by asking questions? In our hurry-up world, we seldom take the time to really hear each other. Could this be one of the reasons many of us feel so disconnected from each other and God?

2. *Give beauty.* Share the flowers and vegetables that grow in your garden with your friends. Tell someone about the mockingbird you heard last evening before you fell asleep. Or just smile at people as you pass them in the hall.

3. *Give kind words.* Thank people when they do something for you—even if it's something they're supposed to do. Thank the vet for taking care of your cat; the cashier at the grocery store for checking you out; the police officer for reminding you that you are driving too fast!

Compliment others on: their brightly colored tie or dress that they chose to wear on a dreary day; a job well done when you needed it in a rush; on always being able to keep the vending machines stocked at work.

Write a note to someone who has been having a difficult time; a neighbor whose yard is particularly lovely or whose children are well-behaved.

4. *Give forgiveness.* Stop holding grudges. Let go of the past and all the bitterness it can produce. If a serious offense committed against you has proven too difficult to release on your own, seek counseling. Remember that forgiveness is a gift you give yourself as well. When you stop fretting about the past or the ill-will someone holds against you, you finally will be able to enjoy the present.

5. *Give laughter.* Laughter draws people together. When we

hear a joke, we immediately want to tell it to someone else. When we hear other people laugh, we gravitate toward them to discover what's so funny. Laughter makes us feel good. And when we feel good, it's easier to experience a sense of faith and joy.

6. *Give a prayer*. We can do this anywhere, anytime, and when all else fails. Tears may choke our laughter or rudeness obscure the beauty lying right in front of us. But nothing ever stands between us and God's ear, for He is the Master Conductor, and He delights to hear us all playing in harmony.

Chapter 9

TOGETHER AT THE WATER'S EDGE

The parable

Youngsters, especially two-year-olds, are experts at asking questions. From the time they get up until the time they are tucked in at night. But Luke 10:25-37 tells us a story about an adult expert who asked what is probably the most famous, the most important, question of all. At least as far as a Christian is concerned. Why should the inquiry "Who is my neighbor?" be such a significant question? Because the story Christ told as an answer is the story of His mission as our Saviour and the story of our mission as His disciples.

As the unexpected good Samaritan, Jesus did not gaze upon us as we lay wounded and bleeding along the treacherous road of sin only to pass us by. Instead, "taking the very nature of a servant . . . he humbled himself and became obedient to death—even death on a cross" in order that He might put us on the road to His kingdom (Phil. 2:7, 8).

The Gospels are full of stories describing Jesus' servant nature. But perhaps John 13:1-17 is the most explicit one. Jesus and His disciples are celebrating their last Passover together. As was common, they would probably be lying on the floor around a low table, propped up on one arm while eating with the other. The feet of one person would be placed behind the head of another. Considering that shoe wear consisted of sandals and that the streets were mere earthen ways, traveled by animals as well as people, the habit of having a servant wash the guests' feet as they entered a house made good sanitary sense. Usually, a child or servant (but never a Jewish servant) would perform this distasteful task. If neither was present, the eldest person in the group would assign the job to the youngest person available. One would assume that the disciples' preparations for this celebration would have included finding a servant to perform this service (Luke 22:7-13). But apparently they did not. Was this an oversight planned by Providence? It would seem so, for John 13:1-5 tells us that Jesus washed the disciples' feet to show "them the full extent of his love."

How Christ's action stood in direct contrast to the bickering that would take place later over who of the disciples was the greatest (Luke 22:24). How His nature stands in direct contrast to Peter's. Drawing attention to himself, Peter proudly asks, "Lord, are *you* going to wash *my* feet?" (John 13:6; emphasis supplied). Jesus humbly deigned to do so in the first place. (Remember, it was a task not even a Jewish *servant* would perform.) Desiring control, Peter boasts, "No, . . . you shall *never* wash my feet" (verse 8; emphasis supplied). But Jesus gave up control the second He humbled Himself by taking the nature of a servant. Peter is leery of giving himself and accepting the service of others. Therefore, he would not serve nor be served by his Master. Jesus, on the other hand, gave of Himself freely when He came to this earth and continued doing so right up to the cross.

Jesus' reply to Peter further clarifies His mission to us. "Unless I wash you, you have no part with me. . . . A person who has had a bath needs only to wash his feet; his whole body is clean. And you are clean, though not every one of you" (verses 8, 10).

These words mean more than bodily cleanliness. Christ is still speaking of the higher cleansing as illustrated by the lower. He who came from the bath was clean, but the sandaled feet soon became dusty, and again needed to be washed. So Peter and his brethren had been washed in the great fountain opened for sin and uncleanness. Christ acknowledged them as His. But temptation had led them into evil, and they still needed His cleansing grace. When Jesus girded Himself with a towel to wash the dust from their feet, He desired by that very act to wash the alienation, jealousy, and pride from their hearts. This was of far more consequence than the washing of their dusty feet. . . . Their hearts must be cleansed. Pride and self-seeking create dissension and hatred, but all this Jesus washed away in washing their feet. A change of feeling was brought about. Looking upon them, Jesus could say, "Ye are clean." Now there was union of heart, love for one another. They had become humble and teachable. Except Judas, each was ready to concede to another the highest place. Now with subdued and grateful hearts they could receive Christ's words.

Like Peter and his brethren, we too have been washed in the blood of Christ, yet often through contact with evil the heart's purity is soiled. We must come to Christ for His cleansing grace. Peter shrank from bringing his soiled feet in contact with the hands of his Lord and Master; but how often we bring our sinful, polluted hearts in contact with the heart of Christ! How grievous to Him is our evil temper, our vanity and pride! Yet all our infirmity and defilement we must bring to Him. He alone can wash us clean.—*The Desire of Ages*, 646, 649.

After Jesus completed washing the disciples' feet, He told them, "Now that I, your Lord and Teacher, have washed your feet, you also should wash one another's feet. I have set you an example that you should do as I have done for you" (verses 14, 15). This, then, is our mission as His disciples. But what does it mean to us today? Because the answer to that question falls in the area of the *Now what?* section appearing at the end of each chapter, we will break with tradition and go directly to that section. (*Elsewhere in the Bible* and *Your story*, therefore, will conclude this chapter.)

Now what?

How about us? Do we fully understand what Christ meant when He said, "You also should wash one another's feet" (verse 14)? Or have these words deteriorated into nothing more than a traditional form, an excuse to stay home from church once every quarter or so? Before you attempt to answer these questions, meditate upon the meaning of Jesus' example and words, for they are as meaningful now as they were then.

Earlier we saw that Peter resisted His Saviour's act of service. But traveling the Christian journey means accepting Jesus as our guide. We must admit we cannot make the journey without His help. If it were not for His salvation, offered to us not because of any merit we possess, but because of what He did for us, we would not even be able to start the journey in the first place. Accepting Christ's service, then, means we are no longer in control; we are stripped of our self-sufficiency and, therefore, our pride. In this age of independence, perhaps it is even more difficult for us than it was for Peter to admit any deficiency on our part. But no matter. Christ's answer is still the same. "Unless I wash you, you have no part with me." In other words, until we learn that being a Christian means receiving Christ's love and grace—His service on our behalf—we cannot really be His disciples. If we are to be like Him, we must relinquish not only our need to be in control, but all efforts to save ourselves. Only then can we serve Him. And only then will our acts of service be responses of gratitude for what He has done on our behalf.

What will such acts of service look like? Jesus tells us in Matthew 25:31-46. Food, clothing, a visit. All are small. But all have major consequences for the person serving as well as for the person receiving. It is such acts and their motivation that determine our standing in the judgment. But why such small acts? Doesn't God value large sums of money donated for building projects? Doesn't He hold in high regard the heart specialist or brain surgeon who saves lives when no other practitioner is able to? Of course He does. But even the person He blesses with such abilities must be ready and willing to perform the so-called less noble acts of service that receive little, if any, glory. Jesus said it Himself when He said, "I tell you the truth, no servant is greater than his master" (John 13:16). As important as the small acts described in Matthew 25:31-46 are, they symbolize more. They are akin to the many acts of stewardship outlined in the *Now what?* section of the previous chapter. And as such, they answer the question faithful stewardship poses, "What can I do for my Saviour?"

There is one last aspect of Jesus' example in John 13 that teaches us about His mission of service and, therefore, ours. He even washed the feet of the disciple who would betray Him to the authorities for the price of a slave. Thus we learn that He desires to assist even those who reject Him and that His service does not designate who of us is worthy of His help. Thank goodness this is so. "For all [of us] have sinned and fall short of the glory of God" (Rom. 3:23). Yet He died that any one of us might be saved (John 3:16).

But how carefully we ration our help. How self-righteously we learn to ignore people who accept our service but not their responsibility. Yet Jesus' response toward Judas portrays the essence of Christian service—humbling oneself to serve the needs of others regardless of the outcome.*

As the unexpected good Samaritan, Jesus rightfully asks us to lay down our pride and pick up the scepter of His kingdom—a scepter called service. This is what we really are agreeing to do when we observe the ordinance of humility. What's your excuse *now* for not attending Communion?

Elsewhere in the Bible

What biblical person gave so generously to others that her name today is synonymous with service? The answer, of course, is Dorcas (Acts 9:32-42). Her motivation? "She was a worthy disciple of Jesus, and her life was filled with acts of kindness. . . . [She] had been of great service to the church. . . ."— *The Acts of the Apostles*, 131, 132. With needles as her tools and her home as her workshop, she teaches us what Christ wants us to learn from His towel and basin of water.

Dorcas lived in Joppa, 34 miles northwest of Jerusalem. Such a location gave her ample opportunities to be a good Samaritan, for Joppa was a major Christian center during the time when Christianity was spreading from Jerusalem across the Mediterranean. From the roof of her mud-brick house, Dorcas could watch the city's poor as they traced their way through life, eking out a living. Perhaps she would make mental notes to stitch a new set of clothes for Simon, the blind beggar, or hem a blanket for Rachel's new baby. Poor little thing. His father's body, washed ashore, along with remnants of his fishing boat just last week.

But then one day, Dorcas became sick and died. We can imagine the care the widows she helped took as they prepared her body for burial. We can imagine how they must have mourned as they made arrangements for her funeral. Picture the two men rushing the ten miles or so to Lydda, hoping Peter would return with them to work a miracle. And so he did. The same Peter who earlier had closed his hands to his Master's service, had learned after all to accept His "cleansing grace." Now these same hands would soon help Dorcas to her feet.

Surely the shouts of joy must have been louder than the wails of sadness as the people Dorcas served sensed a new joy. She who had raised the spirits of so many from a living death, had been raised from physical death. And so shall it be with us and those we have served. If not now, then when Christ returns to say, "Inherit the kingdom prepared for you from the foundation of the world. . . . Just as you did it to one of the least of these who are members of my family, you did it to me" (Matt. 25:34, 40, NRSV).

Your story

This *Your story* section includes two short narratives (once again breaking with tradition!) written by two different individuals. The first writer tells us what it meant to have good Samaritans appear just when she needed them most.

"I was a single Mom living with my three children in a new, low-income Farm Home Administration house. Because they were worried about low-income housing being built on their block, my neighbors were anxious that I maintain the appearance of both the house and yard. I worked two jobs to support my family and had little time or money for yardwork and general maintenance. One day, a spring on my garage door came unhooked, causing the door to sway lop-sidedly. The man across the street told me I must do something about this eyesore!

"I had just become a newly-baptized member of the local Seventh-day Adventist Church. The Sabbath after the garage door broke, many of the other members invited my children and me to attend a church picnic on Sunday. As much as we wanted to go, I declined the invitation, explaining that I had to repair my garage door. Actually, I was only planning to prop the one side up with bricks so it would at least look straight from the street.

"When Sunday morning came around, my daughter called out to me. 'Look, Mom. Here come the Miller family. Mr. Kline is with them, too. And he's carrying a heavy tool box.' When I went to greet them, they said they had come to repair my door! Bonnie Miller had brought some refreshments for the children and me. So while the men worked, we sat under the shade of a tree and got better acquainted.

"In about an hour, the garage door was as good as new, and it was only 9:00 a.m. The church picnic wouldn't begin until noon. Bonnie stated that she had prepared plenty of food for my family, too, hoping that we would change our minds.

"I was overwhelmed by such generosity. I had been a single parent for over ten years. Yet no one ever had offered to do so much for me, especially in one day. We went to the picnic and had a wonderful time. I was so happy to have found a 'real church family' to belong to!"

The final story comes from the person who wrote the *Your story* section for chapter 5. As you read it, think about how helping each other to the water's edge is the same as being a good Samaritan.

"A small but expectant audience had assembled for the healing service. What had brought each of us here? Was it to be healed of physical maladies or long-standing emotional wounds? Was it for the 'laying on of hands'? Or to support a friend or family member? Regardless, I felt that the sanctuary was a collective void containing many vessels, each waiting to be filled. And I was but one of them.

"The Scripture was from the Gospel of John—the lame man by the pool of Bethesda and how he was healed simply by the word of Jesus. As I listened to the verses, I wondered about this miracle. I thought of the man who was healed and how his life was changed by just the words, 'Take up your bed and walk.' The sermon for the evening sprang from these words. And it was clear that the pastor had meditated long upon the passage that contained them, the concept of healing, and the desperately sick world in which we live. Thus she asked the questions, 'What do we heal?' and 'How do we begin to heal?'

"She shared her picture of a healing community, stating that we might all be healed and all be healers at the same time. 'Ours is a world of pain and aloneness, disease and suffering. We can each love those with whom we come in contact, sharing with them some of the strength we have received through our connection with the Great Healer. We can help them down to the metaphorical pool, to where the healing waters are.'

"Then she pointed out that it is the trip to the water together that counts. If we help each other to the water's edge, with faith and with love, we all will benefit from the healing process. We all will find peace.

"As the healing groups assembled in the four corners of the sanctuary, carefully selected background music spoke further of healing with words such as: 'He brought me to the banqueting house, and His banner over me is love,' and 'There is a Balm in Gilead, to heal the sin-sick soul.'

"Specific requests were offered. Faith was expressed. Arms were interlocked in loving support. And God's love, presence, and healing power were sought. As I stood there, wrapped in love and support, I felt the fullness I had come seeking. The sanctuary seemed full of God's healing power. He had found this tiny room, in a building, in a city filled with noise and bustle, in a world filled with disregard and pain. His love and power abode as we had come together to the water's edge."

* When does such help become enabling, as in substance abuse cases? This can be decided only on an individual basis. Remember that at times the best help may be no help or a strong intervention program in which the person realizes that his or her behavior is destroying not only his or her life, but the lives of others as well.

Chapter 10

IN THE PRESENCE OF GOD

The parable

After the Civil War in the United States, the Confederate General, Robert E. Lee, visited a woman who showed him the skeletal remains of an ancient tree that once stood as a sentinel before her house. "Enemy artillery did this," she wept bitterly, hoping Lee would denounce such an act or at least sympathize with her. But all Lee would say was, "Cut it down, my dear Madam, and forget it."

How much better off we all would be if we were to "cut down" the injustices done to us rather than continue to condemn the enemy who committed them. Jesus' parable in Matthew 18:21-35 teaches us at least three major points about forgiveness that make this so. Two of these points will be discussed in this section. The third one will be taken up in the *Now what?* section, which, once again breaking with tradition, will immediately follow.

Point number 1 is this: *God's forgiveness helps us develop a more profound awareness of the gravity of sin and the magnitude of His grace.* In verses 23-27, we read about a servant who owed his king ten thousand talents, quite a ridiculous sum considering that even King Herod's yearly paycheck probably amounted to only nine hundred talents! In fact, it was such a ridiculously large sum the servant couldn't possibly pay it. But rather than sell him, the king had compassion on him and freed him from his enormous debt.

93

Such is the extent of the forgiveness God bestows upon us. Our sin is so great a debt—it caused the death of His Son—there is nothing we can do to repay Him. But if He were not willing to forgive us, we would surely be purchased by another, a far less merciful master.

But God's forgiveness does more than merely cancel our debt. Just as the servant was able to continue with the king once the king canceled his debt, so God's forgiveness (coupled, of course, with our repentance) enables us to be reconciled to Him. Thus the story of the unmerciful servant becomes yet another story of God's love and grace.

Once our awareness of the gravity of sin and the magnitude of God's grace has increased, we start learning what it means to forgive others from the heart (verse 35). Peter's question prompting the parable (verse 21) was based on righteousness by works. But those who forgive "from the heart" reflect on the mercy of their heavenly Father and can therefore do likewise toward their fellow humans.—Adapted from *SDA Bible Commentary*, 5:450. Such acts of mercy are a result of righteousness by faith and portray true forgiveness.

Second, *God's forgiveness requires that we forgive those who have injured us.* One would surely think that because the king had forgiven the servant such an enormous sum, the servant would have been inclined to do likewise with someone who owed him. But in verses 28-30, we learn that the exact opposite happened. Indeed, he could not even forgive someone who owed him 500,000 times *less* than the debt he had owed! Knowing that God has forgiven us a debt impossible to repay, how can we not forgive others their debts against us?

The fact that we are under so great obligation to Christ places us under the most sacred obligation to those whom He died to redeem. We are to manifest toward them the same sympathy, the same tender compassion and unselfish love, which Christ has manifested toward us. . . .

Our Saviour taught His disciples to pray: "Forgive us our debts, as we forgive our debtors." A great blessing is here asked upon conditions. We ourselves state these conditions. We ask that the mercy of God toward us may be measured by the mercy which we extend to others. Christ declares that this is the rule by which the Lord will deal with us. "If ye forgive men their trespasses, your heavenly Father will also forgive you; but if ye forgive not men their trespasses, neither will your Father forgive your trespasses." Wonderful terms! But how little are they understood or heeded. One of the most common sins, and one that is attended with most pernicious results, is the indulgence of an unforgiving spirit. How many will cherish animosity or revenge and then bow before God and ask to be forgiven as they forgive. Surely they can have no true sense of the import of this prayer or they would not dare to take it upon their lips. . . . If, in all their daily intercourse, Christians would carry out the principles of this prayer, what a blessed change would be wrought in the church and in the world! This would be the most convincing testimony that could be given to the reality of Bible religion.—*Testimonies for the Church*, 5:170, 171.

Verses 31-35 teach us why this second point is so important. God will forgive us the same way we have forgiven others. Matthew 5:7 says it this way: "Blessed are the merciful, for they will be shown mercy." And James 2:13 states: "Judgment without mercy will be shown to anyone who has not been merciful. Mercy triumphs over judgement!" If we have been merciful in our dealings with others, we need not fear the judgment, for God will be merciful to those who have been merciful themselves.

Now what?

But how will God's requirement that we forgive those who have injured us affect our life? How will it draw us closer to Him? The answers stem from the third major point about forgiveness taught in Jesus' parable: *Forgiving others will cost us.* We cannot change the fact that someone has harmed us, that we want to "get even."

But forgiveness means forgetting what happened and letting go of the right we think is ours to see justice prevail. Forgiveness means that we will learn to care more about the person and less about what she or he has done until we don't care about it at all. Of course forgetting and letting go is never easy. Forgiving another person may be about the most difficult thing any of us has ever had to do. Especially when it is a church member who has wronged us—someone who should have known better. But when the ghosts of past offenses haunt our hearts, it helps to remember that Jesus has forgiven us more than we could repay. It also helps to remember that most likely someone, somewhere, is trying to forget something you have done to them. Wouldn't you hope they could?

Forgiving and letting go sets us free. And the freedom is worth the cost. When we stop "seeking revenge" and "feeling wounded," when we stop blaming and condemning the other person for how miserable she or he has made us, we are better able to enjoy life, plus have more meaningful friendships and a deeper relationship with God.

> God's whole attitude is one of forgiving love. He sends his rain on the just and the unjust and makes the sun shine on the evil and the good. Out of His love He sent into the world His own Son. Not only does He wait for men to come humbly and contritely asking forgiveness. In Jesus He goes to find them and offer them His love. If we are dominated by bitterness, if in our hearts there is a little chapel of hate, if we say, "I can never forgive and I can never forget," then the principle of our life is diametrically opposed to the principle of the life of God. Therefore if we would enter into real fellowship with God we must learn by His grace to forgive as He forgives.—William Barclay, *And Jesus Said* (Philadelphia, Pa.: The Westminster Press, 1970), 91.

Elsewhere in the Bible

Surely Stephen was a person who learned to live by God's grace, forgiving even as He forgives. We first meet Stephen in

Acts 6 when the twelve disciples choose him to be one of the seven deacons who would help distribute food to the widows of the church. He is the only one of the seven the Bible describes as being "full of faith and of the Holy Spirit" (verse 5). Immediately afterward, we read that Stephen "did great wonders and miraculous signs among the people" (verse 8). So it would seem that he went miles beyond his original responsibility as deacon.

Unfortunately, Stephen's wonders and signs caused great concern among the Hebrew religious leaders. They leveled false charges of blasphemy against him—charges punishable by death (verses 9-15). Soon he found himself defending Christ and His gospel before the Sanhedrin (chapter 7), a defense that so angered these experts that they fell upon him, dragged him from the city, and stoned him (verses 54-59).

How untimely Stephen's death seems to have been. He had just been appointed deacon. And he seemed to have been reaching his stride as a great preacher and miracle worker. Yet it does not appear that it was any of this work that provided the greatest testimony. Instead, it was Stephen's vision and death (verses 56-60) that

> testified to the reality of the life beyond this life with Jesus and the angels. His vision robbed the terror from his dying [and ours], and because of his death we learn that martyrdom is sometimes necessary for the conversion of a soul. By Stephen's murder Saul became Paul, and the Christian church incurred a debt it will never be able to repay. His loving prayer echoes across the chasms of dark ignorance and sharp bigotry, "Lord, lay not this sin to their charge," and moves our hearts today.—Leslie Hardinge, *The Victors* (Nampa, Idaho: Pacific Press Publishing Association, 1982), 18.

Filled with the Holy Spirit not only when appointed to a position of high standing within the church, but also when asked to die for Christ (verse 60), Stephen's last act and words echoed those spoken by Christ in the greatest story of forgiveness ever told (Luke 23:34). Do our words and deeds echo the same?

Your story

How could he say those things about me? Tim wondered. *How could he accuse me of doing those things when he knew full well I hadn't?* Tim's story portrays the usual cycle: Someone does something to you that hurts terribly. First, you can't believe it. Then you are dismayed by it. The anger grows until it governs your life. Unfortunately for many of us, the story ends there. But, thankfully for Tim, he found the strength to "cut down his tree" and forget about it. He continues:

"When we were in academy, Bill and I were both vying for the affections of the same girl. One day, however, she and I decided we weren't suited for each other and parted friends. That summer, we even colporteured together. When I started selling a lot of books, she would occasionally seek me out for advice and encouragement. Meanwhile, she and Bill continued to date and eventually decided to get married. But why I'll never know, he always spoke ill of me. In fact, he even accused me of doing things I never would have dreamed of doing.

"Because it was all so damaging, I couldn't bring myself to 'forgive and forget.' I couldn't leave it in God's hands to prevent or undo any damage that might occur because of Bill's words. After awhile, however, I began to realize that my relationship with God had grown stagnant. My prayers didn't seem to be going any farther than the proverbial ceiling, regardless of how I prayed, when I prayed, or what I prayed for. My anger and resentment toward Bill, however, seemed to be flourishing. Whenever I went to church, I wondered whose ears Bill's words had reached. *Maybe I should stop coming*, I thought one Sabbath while listening to the prelude.

"Then one day another thought came to me, *It doesn't matter what Bill thinks or says about you.* I tried dismissing it, because the point to me was that it *did* matter. Bill had never asked me to forgive him, so why should I? But the thought nagged on like a dripping faucet. Finally, I decided to fix it. As I knelt in prayer, I asked God to help me forgive Bill. I didn't particularly feel any different when I arose. But over the course of the next few days, I awakened to the fact that I had been brooding less and less. My prayers seemed to have taken on a new vitality. And I even had more physical energy. That Sabbath as I crossed the threshold of the sanctuary, I realized it no longer mattered that a fellow church member might have been the recipient of Bill's slander against me. And it was then that I also realized I had crossed the threshold of another sanctuary. To forgive another is truly to be in the presence of God."

Chapter 11

ANGELS IN THE KITCHEN

The parables

Bartolomé Esteban Murillo (1618-1682) was one of Spain's greatest painters. The Louvre, in Paris, is home to his painting *The Miracle of San Diego*. In this painting, a door opens, and three men enter a bustling kitchen where each kitchenmaid is busy with an appointed task. One maid is carrying a waterpot, while another is tending a basket of vegetables. A third one is coaxing a fire. But all the maids have one thing in common—Murillo depicted them as angels! The message of this masterpiece is part of the message Jesus expressed in the parables of Luke 12:35-40 and Matthew 25:35-40. Doing the task at hand, no matter how minor it seems, is equal to serving Him if it is done in response to His love for us. A cup of cold water, a loaf of bread, a visit to one of society's castoffs, waiting to open the gate for your master even during an hour when he is not likely to return, or guarding the master's property from intruders—all symbolize the duty we have while waiting for Christ to return—caring for and protecting that which He has placed in our charge.

From day to day, month to month, or even year to year, God gives all of us specific charges that He hopes we will tend to. Most of these charges fall under general categories that include our relationship to people, the gospel, the commandments and the testimony of Jesus, and nature.

1. *Our relationship to people.* There is no question about it.

We cannot live without coming into contact with others. And, in a sense, all whose lives we touch are a charge given to us by God. Regardless of whether they believe in Him or not, He created them. Should there be any question then, about how we treat them? The gas station attendant sitting in a smoky booth, the harried department store clerk on a sale day, the waitress whose feet hurt, everyone we meet during our day, deserves to be treated with dignity and respect. A Thank you, a friendly Hello, or patience when the cash register jams could be the refreshing drink someone is waiting for. "Be tenderhearted, be courteous" (1 Pet. 3:8, NKJV).

But what about those people who "drive us crazy," many of whom we could classify as less than friendly? Christ's advice still rings true: "For if you love those who love you, what reward do you have? Do not even the tax collectors do the same? And if you greet only your brothers and sisters, what more are you doing than others? Do not even the Gentiles do the same? Be perfect, therefore, as your heavenly Father is perfect" (Matt. 5:46-48, NRSV).

> **Perfect** [verse 48]. . . . Jesus does not here deal with absolute sinlessness in this life. . . .
>
> The Jews were toiling wearily to become righteous by their own efforts, to earn salvation by works. But in their scrupulous legalism they paid so much attention to the minute details of the letter of the law that they lost sight completely of its spirit. . . . They had made the law an end in itself, something to be kept for its own sake, and had forgotten that its purpose was to lift their gaze to the high ideals of supreme love toward God and self-sacrificing love toward one's fellow men.— *SDA Bible Commentary*, 5:341.

Scripture abounds with verses dealing with this high ideal of self-sacrificing love, only a few of which are listed below. As you read them, remember that they are God's instructions regarding the service we perform for others while awaiting His return. (See Proverbs 14:31; 29:7; Ezekiel 16:49; Zechariah 7:9, 10; Romans 12:9-21; 13:8-10; 14; 15; 1 Peter 4:7-10).

2. *Our relationship to the gospel.* Martin of Basle and Martin Luther came to an understanding of righteousness by faith about the same time. Because Martin of Basle was cautious about making a public confession, he wrote the following and stuffed it behind a loose stone in his wall. No one discovered it for over one hundred years: "O most merciful Christ, I know that I can be saved only by the merit of thy blood. Holy Jesus, I acknowledge thy sufferings for me. I love thee! I love thee!" Martin Luther, however, said, "My Lord has confessed me before men; I will not shrink from confessing Him before kings." History has written the rest of his story.

Which of the two Martins are you most like? Jesus may have given the gospel commission of Matthew 28:18-20 to His twelve disciples just before He ascended to heaven. But Matthew 5:13-16 plainly teaches that it is a charge given to all who follow Him.

> The Saviour's words, "Ye are the light of the world," point to the fact that He has committed to His followers a world-wide mission. In the days of Christ, selfishness and pride and prejudice had built strong and high the wall of partition between the appointed guardians of the sacred oracles and every other nation on the globe. But the Saviour had come to change all this. The words which the people were hearing from His lips were unlike anything to which they had ever listened from priest or rabbi. Christ tears away the wall of partition, the self-love, the dividing prejudice of nationality, and teaches a love for all the human family. He lifts men from the narrow circle that their selfishness prescribes; He abolishes all territorial lines and artificial distinctions of society. He makes no difference between neighbors and strangers, friends and enemies. He teaches us to look upon every needy soul as our neighbor and the world as our field.—*Thoughts From the Mount of Blessing*, 42.

Acts of courtesy and kindness, Bible studies, evangelistic meetings, Christian educational and medical institutions, plus radio and television programs, are all lights set on a hill. And waiting for His return means being involved in some or all of these in some way.

But being involved in the gospel commission is more than bringing people to Jesus. It also includes nurturing not only the young in Christ, but the supposedly established church members as well. It is bearing one another's burdens, helping each other keep our eyes on Christ as we travel the Christian journey together.

3. *Our relationship to the commandments of God and the testimony of Jesus*. Revelation 12:17 and 19:10 tell us that while waiting for Christ's return, we are made charges of His commandments and the testimony of Jesus. The early Seventh-day Adventist Church did a more than admirable job in restoring the Ten Commandments and the gift of prophecy to its rightful place in the structure of Christianity. To honor our church's founding mothers and fathers, let us never forget the great laws upon which the Ten Commandments were established (Matt. 22:34-40) and that Ellen White herself said, "The written testimonies are not given to give new light, but to impress vividly upon the heart the truths of inspiration already revealed."— *Testimonies for the Church*, 5:665.

We dishonor those who have traveled the path before us when we use these charges as clubs to pommel those who do not believe or who supposedly have gone astray (most often from our own cherished opinions and/or traditions). Instead, they should serve to soften our own hearts, melt our own frozen attitudes in preparation for taking charge of our own responsibility within the gospel commission.

4. *Our relationship to nature*. Isaiah links ecological problems with our relationship to God's commands: "The earth dries up and withers. . . . The earth lies polluted under its inhabitants; for they have transgressed laws, violated the statutes, broken the everlasting covenant" (24:4, 5, NRSV).

As Christians, we learn to treat the Bible with respect. If you grew up in a Christian home, your mother or father probably taught you not to stuff papers in it, bend its covers back, or stack other books on top of it. Because nature teaches us much about God as well, why would we want to abuse it? Yet that is what many of us do every day in a rather mindless fashion, regardless of the first command God gave humankind. "Be fruitful and increase in number; fill the earth and subdue it. Rule over the fish of the sea and the birds of the air and over every living creature that moves on the ground" (Gen. 1:28). This command gives us the privilege of using the earth's resources for our necessities (see *SDA Bible Commentary*, 1:217). But it does not give us the right to violate that which God has created for the purpose of sustaining life, giving us pleasure, and teaching us about Himself.

> "God is love" is written upon every opening bud, upon every spire of springing grass. The lovely birds making the air vocal with their happy songs, the delicately tinted flowers in their perfection perfuming the air, the lofty trees of the forest with their rich foliage of living green—all testify to the tender, fatherly care of our God and to His desire to make His children happy.—*Steps to Christ*, 10.

Taking care of the earth is one way of recognizing that even though God put us in charge of it, He was the one who created it and therefore owns it. We are merely stewards of it and as such

> should do everything to maintain life on all levels by keeping the ecological balance intact. In His coming advent, Christ will "destroy those who destroy the earth" (Rev. 11:18). From this perspective Christian stewards are responsible not only for their own possessions but for the world around them.—*Seventh-day Adventists Believe . . .* , 274.

Elsewhere in the Bible

When Paul became a Christian, he took seriously the charge we all have received in Matthew 28:18-20. The book of Acts overflows with stories of how he helped to spread God's love and grace. One of these is found in chapter 16:6-15. Spurred on to Europe by a vision, Paul, Timothy, and Silas traveled to Philippi. The next Sabbath, they attended a worship service conducted by women, one of whom was Lydia, a business person dealing in fabrics. The phrase *a worshiper of God* used in verse 14 to describe her tells us that she "had accepted Judaism to the extent of worshiping Jehovah" (*SDA Bible Commentary*, 6:246). Now God was providing an opportunity for her to take the next step. And indeed, "the Lord opened her heart to respond to Paul's message" (verse 14). She and her household, most likely composed of servants and business employees, were baptized. One would assume that the story ends there, for the account immediately gives way to another in which Paul and Silas release a girl from devils. Because she had been serving as a medium, her masters could no longer reap the monetary benefits of her former "abilities." Thus they started a riot against Paul and Silas that landed them in prison. When an earthquake rescued them from their cell, where did they go? To Lydia's house (verse 40). And instead of reasoning that her association with these "criminals" might affect her business, she admitted them to fellowship with their brothers and sisters in Christ.

And so the church in Europe was born from one person taking up the responsibility God gave him. Lydia also accepted her responsibility toward the gospel as she provided space and an encouraging atmosphere in which the first European church could flourish. They did not know at the time that once again history would change its course because of doing so. But they did so anyway. Was Lydia alive when Paul wrote his letter to the church in Philippi, a letter he might never have written if not for her?

Many of you may be thinking that you are not Paul, that you cannot do such great things as he. But that is not the point of the parables that began this chapter. Small duties, small courtesies, performed out of love for the Saviour while we wait for Him to return, make big differences. It was no great thing Paul did when he looked for a place to pray and worship that Sabbath. And it was natural for him to share his love for Christ with the worshipers he found. This is how the stories of God's love and grace can change a life, and in turn, the world.

Your story

The account in this section is just one example of what Christians are doing all over the world to take care of what God has placed in their charge while they await His second coming. After you finish reading it, think about what people near you are doing in any one of the categories discussed in *The parable* section. Then consider what you have been doing or what you could do in the future.

"We purchased our new house in a subdivision where mature trees had been bulldozed to make room for 'progress.' But it was all we could afford," write Marianne and Gary. "We've always enjoyed nature, and weather permitting, Sabbath afternoons usually found us bird-watching or hiking. So it was typical for us to want to landscape our half acre with trees, flowers, and shrubs that would attract the birds and little animals that used to live there to begin with. Over the years, we planted groupings of white pines, along with berry-yielding bushes and trees. One spring, Gary decided he wanted to build a water garden complete with koi and a small waterfall. That autumn, we even gathered fallen twigs from a nearby woods to construct a small brush pile in back of our toolshed. In addition, we erected three bird feeders in various parts of the yard.

"It's been thirteen years since we first started designing, digging, and medicating our aching muscles. But even though the transformation was slow, it has been steady and amazing. Last winter, during the holidays, the Lord gifted us with a flock of Eastern bluebirds that stayed for a day to feed on the berries that adorned the blue rug junipers surrounding our water garden. This spring, during the migratory season, we counted forty-eight species of birds in our backyard alone. We even had a blue heron dine on a few of our koi! And this summer, we are watching a clutch of bunnies grow from infancy to adulthood. They seek refuge in the brush pile when our dogs are out and about. Now on Sabbath afternoons, we quite often just stay home and enjoy the miracle of our garden. As we do, we think of the many parables Jesus based on nature. But now He is able to teach us lessons of His love and grace right in our own backyard. Recently, one of our neighbors asked us why we took such an interest in nature. How excited we were to be able to share our belief in God, that He created the earth, and that through His creation, we can learn a lot about Him. Maybe someday this neighbor will have his own story about God's grace to tell!"

Now what?

The parables in Luke 12:35-40 and Matthew 25:35-40 teach us that while waiting for Christ to return we are responsible for certain charges He places upon us and that these responsibilities largely involve our relationship to people, the gospel, the commandments and the testimony of Jesus, and God's creation. But what preparation is necessary for us to meet these responsibilities?

> In all who are under the training of God is to be revealed a life that is not in harmony with the world, its customs, or its practices; and everyone needs to have a personal experience in obtaining a knowledge of the will of God. We must individually hear Him speaking to the heart. When every other voice is hushed, and in quietness we wait before Him, the silence of the soul makes more distinct the voice of God. He bids us, "Be still, and know that I am God." Ps. 46:10. Here alone can true rest be found. And this is the effectual preparation for all who labor for God. Amid the hurrying throng, and the strain of life's intense activities, the soul that is thus refreshed will be surrounded with an atmosphere of light and peace. The life will breathe out fragrance, and will reveal a divine power that will reach men's hearts.—*The Desire of Ages*, 363.

Christ Himself engaged in the spiritual discipline of solitude (Luke 5:16; 6:12; Matt. 14:13, 23; 17:1-9; 26:36-46; Mark

1:35; 6:31). But perhaps His greatest example is found in Matthew 4:1-11, when after His baptism He retreated to the wilderness "to be alone, to contemplate His mission and work. By fasting and prayer He was to brace Himself for the bloodstained path He must travel" (*The Desire of Ages*, 114).

We can learn much from Jesus' special time of solitude.

1. He sought a solitary place after being baptized before a throng of onlookers and after hearing God's magnificent confirmation that He was His Son. Alone in the wilderness, He could put this occasion into perspective. We, too, should seek solitude with God to put our exciting times of service in perspective. Alone with Him, He can remind us that we serve according to His desire and not our own. That His love and Spirit motivate us, not our greedy human need for fame and fortune.

2. The Spirit led Him to the wilderness. So should we be led into solitude. Does this mean we engage in the discipline of solitude only when we feel like it? Did Jesus really think that bracing "Himself for the bloodstained path" was going to be a gala festivity? It is precisely those times when we do not feel like entering into solitude with God that the Spirit is leading and working the hardest on our behalf. Then gather your willpower and go.

3. And while you are there, remember that Jesus stayed long to wrestle with His own humanity.

> Many look on this conflict between Christ and Satan as having no special bearing on their own life; and for them it has little interest. But within the domain of every human heart this controversy is repeated. Never does one leave the ranks of evil for the service of God without encountering the assaults of Satan.—*The Desire of Ages*, 116.

Thus we learn that times of solitude with God may cause grave discomfort as we pit the desires and goals we have for our life against His will for our life.

4. But we can emerge fulfilled from our practice of solitude just as Jesus did. In this special example, as in all the others,

He "gained the victory through submission and faith in God" (*The Desire of Ages*, 130), a submission and faith we gain only by drawing close in silence. Thus in silence, we are made ready to serve until we can be together with Him in the second-coming clouds, our service on this earth complete.

Chapter 12

BEING ON THE ALERT

The parable

When the telegraph was a major source of communication, a group of job applicants were waiting to interview for the job of telegraph operator for a company. As they waited nervously in the office reception area, one of them suddenly jumped up and dashed into the employer's office. When he returned a few minutes later, he exclaimed, "I got the job!" When the others questioned him, he revealed his secret to success. "If you had been paying attention to the dots and dashes coming across the loudspeaker while we were waiting, you would have noticed that the message said, 'The man I need must always be on the alert. The first one who interprets this and comes directly into my office will be hired.' "

In Matthew 25:1-13, Jesus tells a parable about the importance of staying alert and being prepared for His second coming. The parable explains three things about His command in verse 13: (1) *what* it means to keep watch, (2) *why* we are to keep watch, and (3) *how* we are to fulfill the command to keep watch.

1. *What it means to keep watch.* Keeping watch is not just sitting around, waiting for something to happen. Notice that verse 4 tells us the wise bridesmaids came prepared with extra oil. Of course, it meant they had more to carry. But in the end, the effort was worth it!

Likewise, we cannot just sit around, waiting for Christ to

return. We must prepare ourselves for the second coming by learning how to let the oil of God's grace keep our love and service for Him shining brightly. Before Christ returns, we must be justified in His righteousness (Rom. 3:21-24), washed from our sins, and renewed in our nature (Titus (3:5). None of this is anything that can be done at the last minute, as we discover from the five foolish bridesmaids.

Keeping watch also means we will be prepared to make the most of the opportunities to serve Him that come our way. Like the person in our opening illustration who got the job, we will "be in touch" with our surroundings. We will always be "on the lookout" for ways to share the love of Christ with others, for ways to fulfill our responsibilities in the four areas discussed in chapter 11.

2. *Why we are to keep watch.* "Therefore keep watch, *because you do not know the day or the hour*" (Matt. 25:13; emphasis supplied). Scripture assures us of Christ's return (Matt. 16:27; 24:27; John 14:1-3; 1 Thess. 4:16, 17; Titus 2:13, 14: Rev. 1:7; etc.). But "no one knows about that day or hour, not even the angels in heaven, nor the Son, but only the Father" (Matt. 24:36). In Acts 1:7, Jesus replied to the disciples when they asked Him if He was going to restore the kingdom of Israel, "It is not for you to know the times or dates the Father has set."

So what are we meant to know? Christ once again directs all His disciples to the work lying before them. "But you will receive power when the Holy Spirit comes on you; and you will be my witnesses in Jerusalem, and in all Judea and Samaria, and to the ends of the earth" (verse 8). As we meet the responsibilities of that work, the power of His Spirit will energize our efforts and animate our lives with the sense of Christ's presence. Thus there will be no delay in the true sense of the word. We already will be dwelling with Christ, for He will be dwelling in our hearts.

3. *How we are to fulfill the command to keep watch.* How do we let the oil of God's grace keep our love and service for Him shining brightly? What will help us make the most of the opportunities that come our way to serve Him? For the answers to these questions, let us once again observe the bridesmaids.

All of them symbolize all the people who claim to be Christ's disciples. But the five wise bridesmaids represent those disciples who recognize the need to continually replenish their supply of grace. The five foolish ones, having lit their lamps, made no arrangements for feeding them and thus represent those disciples who make little or no effort to nurture the life of grace they once began. None of us can presume we will make it to the second coming without doing so.

We are talking here about abiding in Christ, a subject He discussed in John 15:1-8 and the subject we will discuss next in the *Now what?* section, which once again immediately follows.

Now what?

If we abide in Christ, nurturing the life of grace we once began, we, like the five wise bridesmaids, will be prepared to meet Him when He returns.

> A continuous abiding in a living connection with Christ is essential for growth and fruitfulness. Occasional attention to matters of religion is not sufficient. Riding high on a wave of religious fervor one day, only to fall low into a period of neglect the next, does not promote spiritual strength. To abide in Christ means that the soul must be in daily, constant communion with Jesus Christ and must live *His* life (Gal. 2:20).—*SDA Bible Commentary*, 5:1042.

How can we be "in daily, constant communion with Jesus Christ," maintaining our spiritual strength? Notice the emphasis on the spiritual disciplines in the quotation below:

> Rest yourself wholly in the hands of Jesus. Contemplate His great love, and while you meditate upon His self-denial, His infinite sacrifice made in our behalf in order that we should believe in Him, your heart will be filled with holy joy, calm peace, and indescribable love. As we talk of Jesus, as we call upon Him in prayer,

our confidence that He is our personal, loving Saviour will strengthen, and His character will appear more and more lovely. . . . We may enjoy rich feasts of love, and as we fully believe that we are His by adoption, we may have a foretaste of heaven. Wait upon the Lord in faith. The Lord draws out the soul in prayer, and gives us to feel His precious love.—*Sons and Daughters of God*, 311.

Thus we see that the spiritual disciplines discussed in the *Now what?* sections of this book are the tools we need to help us apply God's stories of love and grace to our own lives. Our use of the disciplines is like the farmer who plants the seed (Mark 4:26-29). He cannot make the seed grow. But in faith, he must cultivate the land and do the planting. We cannot, through any wisdom or power of our own, make God's grace grow in our heart. But through faith, we can use the spiritual disciplines to cultivate our heart-soil so that when "the Spirit of God breathes on the soul, the hidden seed springs up, and at last bears fruit to the glory of God."—*Christ's Object Lessons*, 65.

As our use of the disciplines help us grow spiritually, we will begin to bear fruit (John 15:5).

What is it to bear fruit? It is not all comprised in coming to meeting once a week, and bearing our testimony in prayer or social meeting. We are to be found day by day abiding in the Vine, and bringing forth fruit, with patience, at our home, in our business; and in every relation in life manifesting the Spirit of Christ. There are many who act as though they thought an occasional connection with Christ was all that was necessary, and that they can be accounted living branches because at times they make confession of Christ. But this is a fallacy. The branch is to be grafted into the Vine, and to abide there, uniting itself to the Vine fiber by fiber, drawing its daily supply of sap and nourishment from the root and fatness of the Vine, until it becomes one with the parent stock. The sap that nourishes the Vine must nourish the branch, and this will be evident in the life of him who is abiding in Christ.—Ellen G. White, "The Conditions of Fruit Bearing," *The Signs of the Times*, 18 April 1892, 8.

We must be careful, however, that our use of the disciplines does not degenerate into mere habit or the observance of rigid, fixed laws by which we live or die. The Pharisee, who in his prayer thanked God he was not like robbers, evildoers, adulterers, and tax collectors, shows us how this can happen (Luke 18:9-14). The nature of his prayer tells us he believed he had done all the spiritual growing he needed to do. For him, the spiritual disciplines had become a flourish of outward ceremonies performed to impress others with his religious maturity.

But fortunately, we have a tax collector himself to teach us what the spiritual disciplines are really for—implements to help us abide in a living connection with Him. If we acknowledge what he acknowledged—that we are sinners in need of His love and grace—we will be able to use them as such.

Elsewhere in the Bible

The world is still in its infancy. Its population consists of two groups: the ancestors of Seth, who sustain their farms around Eden, and the descendants of Cain, who are building and settling the cities of Nod. New metal alloys are making the lives of everyone easier, causing the economy to prosper. Such is the setting for quite a short story tucked away in the somewhat tedious account of Adam's genealogy: "When Enoch had lived 65 years, he became the father of Methuselah. And after he became the father of Methuselah, Enoch walked with God 300 years and had other sons and daughters. Altogether, Enoch lived 365 years. Enoch walked with God; then he was no more, because God took him away" (Gen. 5:21-24). The point of this short story resides in the even shorter phrase: "Enoch walked with God." This expression

portrays a life of singularly elevated piety, not merely the constant realization of the divine presence or even a continued effort at holy obedience, but *maintenance of the most intimate relations with God.*—*SDA Bible Commentary*, 1:246; emphasis supplied.

After the birth of his son, as he saw the world grow increasingly wicked, Enoch learned what it meant to abide with His Creator, to maintain "the most intimate relations with God."

> The infinite, unfathomable love of God through Christ became the subject of his meditations day and night; and with all the fervor of his soul he sought to reveal that love to the people among whom he dwelt.
>
> Enoch's walk with God was not in a trance or a vision, but in all the duties of his daily life. He did not become a hermit, shutting himself entirely from the world; for he had a work to do for God in the world. In the family and in his intercourse with men, as a husband and father, a friend, a citizen, he was the steadfast, unwavering servant of the Lord. . . .
>
> There are few Christians who would not be far more earnest and devoted if they knew that they had but a short time to live, or that the coming of Christ was about to take place. But Enoch's faith waxed the stronger, his love became more ardent, with lapse of centuries. . . .
>
> Enoch . . . spent much time in solitude, giving himself to meditation and prayer. Thus he waited before the Lord, seeking a clearer knowledge of His will, that he might perform it. To him prayer was as the breath of the soul; he lived in the very atmosphere of heaven.—*Patriarchs and Prophets*, 84, 85.

One of Enoch's contemporaries was Lamech (Gen. 4:18-24). This descendant of Cain stands in direct contrast to Enoch. Not only was he the first polygamist, but he committed a murder that he boasted about in a song. Did Lamech hear Enoch's words recorded in Jude 14, 15? "See, the Lord is coming with thousands upon thousands of his holy ones to judge everyone, and to convict all the ungodly of all the ungodly acts they have done in the ungodly way, and of all the harsh words ungodly sinners have spoken against him." If he did, surely this prophecy must have struck a chord of terror. But Enoch's story, along with that of the bridesmaids' in Matthew 25, explains that keeping watch and abiding in Christ is to face the day of His coming with confidence, believing that when He returns, He will take us to be with Him just as He did Enoch.

Your story

"If I was 'doing something for God,' I thought I was abiding in Christ," Bill explained. 'Consequently, I often found myself working at the church not only on Sabbath, but during the week as well. If light bulbs needed changing, I was climbing the ladder. If the lawn needed tending, I was pulling weeds. If snowdrifts needed clearing, I was swinging a shovel. Over the years, I had been deacon, elder, Sabbath School teacher, Sabbath School superintendent . . . looking back, the list seems endless. I can't think of anything I haven't done. But then during a particularly heated church-board meeting, I received a rather rude awakening. I had been heavily involved in a particular church project that was proving to be quite a trial. There was little support for the project, and funds were running low. Unfortunately, tempers were running high.

"During the course of the debate, someone really gave me a verbal beating, even going so far as to imply the misappropriation of money. I was stunned. Here I had been trying so hard to steer this project toward a successful completion. Couldn't this person see how much effort I had been extending? How could he say things to me in front of the entire board? If this was the way he felt, why hadn't he come to me personally to settle the matter in private?

"Driving home was a struggle, as bitter thoughts raced through my head. *After everything I've done for the church, and this is the thanks I get! How could You let this happen, Lord? Everything I did, I did for You. And this is how You repay me?* Then I realized something frightening yet wonderful. I had been so busy all those years 'doing the Lord's work' that I had spent little or no time with the 'Lord of the work.' My prayers consisted of short morning and evening 'quickies,' something to be done before leaving the house or turning out the lights, much like brushing my teeth or combing my hair. The only studying I ever did was taking a cursory look at the Sabbath School lesson Friday evening so I'd know what everyone else was talking about. I hardly ever took time for personal devotions. The result? The oil in my lamp had run dry, and I had nothing in reserve. Nothing with which to light my way through this darkness that had descended upon me.

"I won't pretend that attending church wasn't difficult for quite awhile after that horrid board meeting. There were many Sabbaths I simply could not find my way there. But over the course of events that ensued, I learned that to truly abide in Christ we need 'daily, constant communion' with Him. Then, when the winds of strife blow, our lamps will not grow dim but will glow brighter set amidst the dark storm clouds."

Chapter 13

WHEN CLOTHES REALLY DID MAKE THE MAN

The parable

When the Russian author Tolstoy was a boy, he felt he was too ugly to ever be happy. So he made a practice of asking God to make him handsome. "If you will do this for me," Tolstoy pleaded, "I will give you all I own now, and all I will own in the future." But as he grew older and the miracle did not occur, he realized that outward beauty was not the only beauty, and certainly not the best. Gradually, he understood that the only beauty worth having lay in the character God desires a person to have.

The story of the wedding garment in Matthew 22: 1-14 helps us to understand the importance of this character.

> By the wedding garment in the parable is represented the pure, spotless character which Christ's true followers will possess. To the church it is given "that she should be arrayed in fine linen, clean and white," "not having spot, or wrinkle, or any such thing." Rev. 19:8. The fine linen, says the Scripture, "is the righteousness of saints." Eph. 5:27. It is the righteousness of Christ, His own unblemished character, that through faith is imparted to all who receive Him as their personal Saviour.—Ellen G. White, *Maranatha*, 78.

If you are to sit at Christ's table, and feast on the provisions he has furnished at the marriage supper of the Lamb [Rev. 19:7, 8], you must have a special garment, called the wedding garment, which is the white robe of Christ's righteousness. Every one who has on this robe is entitled to enter the city of God; and if Jesus had not been very desirous you should have a place in the mansions he has gone to prepare for those who love him, he would not, at so great an expense to himself, have made all these arrangements that you might be happy and sit at his table and enjoy the home he has gone to prepare for his redeemed family.—Ellen G. White, "The Robe of Christ's Righteousness," *The Youth's Instructor*, 11 August 1886.

Now that we have established the importance of the wedding garment, let us examine it carefully, thread by thread. As we do, we will notice four strong filaments in particular.

1. *The wedding garment symbolizes the imprint of God's grace on our lives.* In the East, the king provided robes for his guests. Therefore, you knew who the king's guests were by their attire. As children of the heavenly Monarch, people will know us by our character, a character given to us by the Monarch Himself. Indeed, it is *His* character. If you say you are a Christian but act no differently than those who do not make such a profession, you are not clothed with the wedding garment. If someone who has lived or worked with you for years has not detected your love for Christ, you are not clothed properly. Or when people associate with you, do they sense something special about you? If you truly possess His character, you will wear the imprint of His grace, and it will motivate all you do and say. Colossians 3:12-14 describes this imprint well:

Therefore, as God's chosen people, holy and dearly loved, clothe yourselves with compassion, kindness, humility, gentleness and patience. Bear with each other and forgive whatever grievances you may have against one another. Forgive as the Lord forgave you. And over

all these virtues put on love, which binds them all
together in perfect unity (Col. 3:12-14).

2. *The wedding garment represents our respect for God.* Out
of respect for their country, people stand as a band plays the
national anthem or when the flag passes by in a parade. When
people are invited to a grand event, they dress in their best to
show how they feel about the person who invited them. So it
was in the parable of the wedding garment. Those whom the
king invited knew they were honored to receive such an invitation. And all except for one expressed their loyalty and thanks
to him by joyfully accepting his wedding garment. The king's
response to this one ungrateful person stands in pointed contrast to this person's attitude. Even though he was rude and
disrespectful to the king, the king still called him friend and
gave him an opportunity to explain his behavior. But the man
was speechless. He had no good reason, not even a sufficient
excuse.

So it is with us who profess Christ. If we love and respect
the King of kings, who died for us on an instrument of torture
reserved for the most vile criminals, we will gladly accept His
white robe of righteousness.

> I will greatly rejoice in the
>   Lord,
> my whole being shall exult in
>   my God;
> for he has clothed me with the
>   garments of salvation,
> he has covered me with the
>   robe of righteousness,
> as a bridegroom decks himself
>   with a garland,
> and as a bride adorns herself
>   with her jewels (Isa. 61:10, NRSV).

He [Christ] says, "If ye keep my commandments, ye
shall abide in my love; even as I have kept my Father's

commandments, and abide in his love. These things have I spoken unto you, that my joy might remain in you, and that your joy might be full" (John 15:10, 11). In Him there is joy that is not uncertain and unsatisfying. If the light that flows from Jesus has come to you, and you are reflecting it upon others, you show that you have joy that is pure, elevating, and ennobling. Why should not the religion of Christ be represented as it really is, as full of attractiveness and power? Why should we not present before the world the loveliness of Christ? Why do we not show that we have a living Saviour, one who can walk with us in the darkness as well as in the light, and that we can trust in Him?— Ellen G. White, *That I May Know Him*, 142.

Do thoughts of Jesus make you as happy as reuniting with an absent friend? Is His presence as welcome as the sun after several days of rain? Do others inquire about your optimism? Then you are taking great delight in wearing Christ's robe of righteousness.

3. *The wedding garment illustrates that we support God's cause.* When the guests in the parable donned the special garments provided for them, they showed their support of and delight in the marriage. They agreed to help, as it were, in the celebration.

How is it with us as professed Christians? Do we agree with the objectives of God's grace and work toward their achievement? Do we rejoice that Christ united with us in order that He might prepare us for the marriage celebration of the Lamb? Then you are wearing the wedding garment and have a seat reserved at that celebration.

4. *The wedding garment signifies our willingness to obey God.* The wedding was a special occasion, and the guests must dress accordingly. The wedding garment given to them was not uncomfortable. But one man felt it an unnecessary nuisance.

As Christians, are we too haughty, too self-willed, too self-reliant to accept God's love and grace? The conditions of acceptance are not like a garment that fits tightly, constraining our movement. "Take my yoke upon you and learn from me, for I am gentle and humble in heart, and you will find rest for you souls. For my yoke is easy and my burden is light" (Matt. 11:29).

When we accept the garment of Christ's character, we are saying we believe Jesus is our substitute, that He bore our sins on the cross, and that we accept His righteousness as our own. We also agree to repent of our sins and turn from them, to pursue a life of holiness by imitating Christ's example with the help of the Holy Spirit. Do others see Christ in you? Then you are wearing the wedding garment.

In the parable, the people who came to the wedding feast were both good and bad (Matt. 22:10). Thus we learn that wearing the white robe of Christ's righteousness does not depend on our past, but on God's love and grace along with our willingness to: (a) accept the imprint of that grace on our lives, (b) respect that grace because of what it led Him to do on our behalf, and (c) support the objectives of that grace.

Elsewhere in the Bible

The story of David's sin and repentance (2 Samuel 11, 12) illustrates the meaning of the parable of the wedding garment for our life today. Victorious against the Syrians and the Ammonites, David felt secure in his role as Israel's king. Perhaps too secure. Remaining in Jerusalem while Joab commanded the army for him, David committed adultery (verses 2-5). When Bathsheba discovered she was pregnant, David plotted to have her husband murdered so the two of them could marry in an attempt to cover up their transgression (verses 14-24).

> It was the spirit of self-confidence and self-exaltation that prepared the way for David's fall. . . . And instead of relying in humility upon the power of Jehovah, he began to trust to his own wisdom and might.— *Patriarchs and Prophets*, 717.

How much David was like the man who refused to wear the king's wedding garment! Pride and self-assurance kept both of them from accepting that which they needed the most. And the king's question, "Friend, . . . how did you get in here without wedding clothes?" (Matt. 22:11) echos Nathan's rebuke of David: "Why did you despise the word of the Lord by doing what is evil in his eyes?" (2 Sam. 12:9). But unlike the improperly clad guest, David admitted his sin against God (verse 13). And because of his repentance, Nathan pronounced not a sentence of condemnation as was the case with the wedding guest, but a sentence of not guilty: "The Lord has taken away your sin"(verse 13).

Turning again to David's words of repentance in Psalm 51, we can imagine God handing him the wedding garment—Christ's perfect white robe of righteous. Observe David's eager acceptance of it. How thankful he is that his wearing such a robe is not dependent upon his gruesome story, but upon God's story of love and grace.

> Cleanse me with hyssop, and I will
>   be clean;
> wash me, and I will be whiter than
>   snow.
> Let me hear joy and gladness;
>   let the bones you have crushed
>   rejoice.
> Hide your face from my sins
>   and blot out all my iniquity.
>
> Create in me a pure heart, O God,
>   and renew a steadfast spirit within
>   me.
> Do not cast me from your presence
>   or take your Holy Spirit from me.
> Restore to me the joy of your salvation
>   and grant me a willing spirit, to
>   sustain me (verses 7-12).

Your story

Ken was eager to share with us the joy he now experiences as a result of accepting the King's wedding garment—Christ's righteousness. Part of his story reminds us that there are many others who long to receive this gift as well:

"As I awake from a restless sleep, my eyes survey my surroundings. A roach scampers around the edge of the cell, hunting for any crumb, however small. The thought of dying looms in my mind like a weight pressing upon me. No matter how hard I try, I cannot escape the knowledge that my time here on death row is limited. I know I am guilty. But no one has ever wanted to live more than I. To have the experience just one more time of wading in a brook, lying in the shade of a tree, or feeling the warmth of the sun on my back!

"Footsteps and the jingling of keys distract my thoughts. It's not mealtime. Could they be coming for me to take that last walk to the death chamber? A key turns in the metal door. I see a guard on the other side of the small glass window. Suddenly he throws the door open wide with no apparent cautionary steps to keep me from bolting. His words ring loud and clear. But I think I must be imagining them, 'You have been pardoned! We are setting you free!' It wasn't until I exchanged my prison garb for clean, new clothes that I realized I was not dreaming!

"This illustration describes in a small way the feeling I had when I came to know Jesus and what His sacrifice on the cross and forgiveness could mean for my life. Recently I met someone else who felt trapped and longed to know the experience of joyous freedom only Christ can give.

"It happened the last night of a six-week series of lectures on spirituality at the Smithsonian Institute in Washington, D.C. When the lecturer asked our class of approximately forty people if we had received what we expected from the course, one man rose and made this statement, 'Not really. Actually I was expecting something else. I was hoping to find something that could fill this terrible void in my life. I have a secure job that I enjoy and a nice home filled with a lovely family. But I feel there is something lacking in my life, and I thought maybe it was something spiritual. I was hoping to find a clue here. But I haven't.'

"Then, looking directly at the instructor, the man queried, 'Do you believe in Jesus Christ?' She stuttered about a bit, and then explained how she had joined a particular church when she was a young girl. When she finished trying to explain her experience, she asked, 'Is there anyone else here who believes and would like to say something?'

"Having already experienced the same feelings of despair as this man, I was able to really identify with his frustration. So I rose to tell him my story. How I felt imprisoned before I learned about Christ. How becoming a Christian when I was forty-eight years old completely changed the rest of my life. And how I have never been bored or lonely since. I explained what I had seen and heard—the testimony of what Jesus had done and is doing in my life. I urged this man never to give up his search for God because He promises that if we seek Him we will find Him.

"My 'conversation' with this person has helped me appreciate anew my own salvation and the hope I have through Jesus. My constant prayer is that he will someday discover Christ and His grace and that I will be seated next to him at the heavenly marriage banquet, listening to the rest of his story."

Now what?

Despite the one man's eviction from the banquet because he failed to wear proper attire, the hall was filled with guests rejoicing in the event and the extension of their king's grace in inviting them and offering them suitable clothing (Matt. 22:10).

Many of Christ's parables contain this same element of joyfulness. The shepherd, along with his friends and neighbors, celebrated when the lost sheep was found (Luke 15:5, 6); the woman asked her friends to rejoice with her when the lost coin reappeared (verse 9); and the father of the prodigal son hosted a festive gathering to honor his son's return (verses 22, 23). The man who found the treasure hidden in the field joyfully sold all he had to purchase it (Matt. 13:44), while those who increased their talents were able to share their master's happiness (25:21).

We can imagine the joy of the tax collector as he experienced the results of his prayer (Luke 18:10-14); the joy of the victim as an enemy rescued him (Luke 10:25-37), and the joy of those on the right of the Son of Man as He invited them to "come . . .

take your inheritance, the kingdom prepared for you since the creation of the world" (25:34). And as we learned in *The parable* section, the wedding garment has a thread of joy woven through it. Even the personal accounts in the *Your story* sections of this book share such an emphasis. Ellen White said it well when she wrote:

> If we are heaven-bound, how can we go as a band of mourners, groaning and complaining all along the way to our Father's house?
> Those professed Christians who are constantly complaining, and who seem to think cheerfulness and happiness a sin, have not genuine religion. . . . These are not in Christ. They are gathering to themselves gloom and darkness, when they might have brightness, even the Sun of Righteousness arising in their hearts with healing in His beams.—*The Ministry of Healing*, 251.

Thus it would seem that celebration as a spiritual discipline is as important as any of the other disciplines. "Rejoice in the Lord always. I will say it again: Rejoice!" (Phil. 4:4). As our personal stories truly begin to reflect God's stories of love and grace, joy will follow as a natural consequence. How can we celebrate this joy?

> Rejoice more in the blessings that we know we have. . . . Let us educate our hearts and lips to speak the praise of God for His matchless love. Let us educate our souls to be hopeful and to abide in the light shining from the cross of Calvary. Never should we forget that we are children of the heavenly King.—*The Ministry of Healing*, 252, 253.

As we learn to follow this advice, time spent with family and friends will become times of celebrating. When we are alone, we will fill the silence with hymns of praise. Beginnings will become even more exciting. Endings will become less sad. And

Sabbath time truly will become the most hallowed time of all.

Let us learn now to celebrate God's love and grace so we can continue doing so at the marriage of the Lamb as His bride who is adorned in His wedding garment—bright and clean (Rev. 19:7, 8). Around that banquet table, there will be room for all and time enough to hear everyone's story. Stories that kept our hope and faith alive, that gave us courage for the journey there. We will tell our stories because God's stories spoke to us and became a part of us. Then as we celebrate God's greatest story around this table, our stories will become a song—the song of the Lamb sung by the redeemed:

> Great and marvelous are your deeds,
>   Lord God Almighty.
> Just and true are your ways,
>   King of the ages.
> Who will not fear you, O Lord,
>   and bring glory to your name?
> For you alone are holy.
> All nations will come
>   and worship before you,
> for your righteous acts have been
>   revealed (Rev. 15:3, 4).

So come. Plan to gather 'round that table, for this reminds me of a story. . . .